I0099857

Preventive and Concomitant Control at Colombia's Supreme Audit Institution

NEW STRATEGIES FOR MODERN CHALLENGES

OECD
BETTER POLICIES FOR BETTER LIVES

Please cite this publication as:
OECD (2021), *Preventive and Concomitant Control at Colombia's Supreme Audit Institution: New Strategies for Modern Challenges*, OECD Public Governance Reviews, OECD Publishing, Paris, *https://doi.org/10.1787/a2bdadf3-en*.

ISBN 978-92-64-92400-0 (print)
ISBN 978-92-64-41757-1 (pdf)

OECD Public Governance Reviews
ISSN 2219-0406 (print)
ISSN 2219-0414 (online)

Foreword

Stemming largely from the historical and structural weaknesses of Colombia's governance system, mismanagement and lack of effective control of public resources have hampered Colombia's socioeconomic progress. A solid integrity system that offers inclusive policies and effective public services and mitigates the risks of corruption is essential to consolidate the rule of law and to reduce poverty and inequality. The COVID-19 crisis has accentuated several of these challenges and increased the relevance of effective and efficient management and control.

To strengthen its integrity system, the supreme audit institution (SAI) of Colombia, the Comptroller General of the Republic (CGR), obtained a new constitutional mandate in 2019. The reform introduced the possibility of exercising a preventive and concomitant control for real-time supervision of the execution of public resources. This is a paradigmatic shift in the way fiscal control is understood and exercised in Colombia.

The CGR asked the OECD to examine the progress made so far, as well as the challenges encountered in the implementation of the new preventive and concomitant control. While identifying areas for improvement and adjustments, the report highlights the added value of this new function and emphasises the untapped potential of the CGR's role in helping change the traditional way of auditing toward a more modern and supportive approach between the SAI and the public administration.

The report builds on the OECD's work and experience in supporting countries in the implementation of the OECD Recommendation on Public Integrity. It provides concrete recommendations to strengthen external control in Colombia, and to ensure that the CGR reform is maintained and leveraged to improve the country's system of control. In addition, the report provides a baseline in relation to preventive and concomitant control and its developments in Latin America, highlighting international experiences of SAIs in this field. The OECD will continue to work with SAIs in the context of its Auditors Alliance, as well as through its audit and risk management reviews, in support of better policies for better lives.

Acknowledgements

The report was prepared by the OECD Public Sector Integrity Division of the Directorate for Public Governance under the leadership of Elsa Pilichowski, OECD Director for Public Governance and Julio Bacio Terracino, Acting Head of the Public Sector Integrity Division. The report was co-ordinated and drafted by Frédéric Boehm and Alice Berggrun, with support and inputs from Laura Uribe. Gavin Ugale, Arturo Rivera Pérez, Miguel Peñailillo, and José Oyola contributed various sections and provided comments. Editorial and administrative support was provided by Meral Gedik, Andrea Uhrhammer, Laura Völker, Charles Victor and Camila Saffirio. The Spanish translation of the report was prepared by Thomas Shah and edited in-depth by the OECD team.

The OECD thanks the Comptroller General of the Republic of Colombia, Luis Felipe Córdoba, and Julián Ruiz, Vice-comptroller General, for their leadership and Paula López for coordinating the project and for all the support provided. The OECD is grateful to all the public officials interviewed at the CGR during this project; in particular, for the discussions with the Directorate of Information, Analysis and Immediate Reaction (DIARI). Finally, the OECD expresses its gratitude to the Government of Colombia, the Secretary of Transparency of the Vice Presidency of the Republic, the Inspector General's Office (PGN) and the Administrative Department of Public Function (DAFP) for their valuable contributions. Special thanks go to the heads of internal control of the national and territorial entities who participated in the two focus groups organized with the help of the DAFP in the framework of this project.

In addition, the report benefited from the reflections and comments of Ricardo Rodríguez Yee, former Vice Comptroller General, Sara Pereira, Ismael Contreras, Luis Fernando Velásquez (*Corporación Acción Ciudadana Colombia*), Manuel Alberto Restrepo Medina (*Universidad del Rosario*) and Andrés Hernández (*Transparencia por Colombia*). Likewise, it had valuable contributions from the IDB Country Office for Colombia, in particular from Francesco de Simone and Juan Carlos Ospina.

Table of contents

FIGURES

TABLES

Follow OECD Publications on:

http://twitter.com/OECD_Pubs

http://www.facebook.com/OECDPublications

http://www.linkedin.com/groups/OECD-Publications-4645871

http://www.youtube.com/oecdilibrary

http://www.oecd.org/oecddirect/

Executive summary

The role of supreme audit institutions (SAIs) has gradually expanded beyond traditional fiscal control. In particular, SAIs can provide critical evidence on what works and what does not work in public governance, and thus inform and promote substantial improvements in public management whilst responding to a crisis of trust in many countries and increasingly complex socioeconomic contexts.

In Colombia, a constitutional reform approved in 2019 gave the Office of the Comptroller General of the Republic (CGR) a preventive and concomitant control function that allows identifying risks and red flags while projects and budgets are being executed. With this new mandate, the CGR can take measures in real time and issue "warnings" and "alerts" to public managers to allow them to take corrective actions, tackle fraud and corruption and thus to meet the expectations of citizens.

Ensuring the effective implementation of the preventive and concomitant control function is crucial to its success. This report reviews the reform and related efforts by the CGR. It identifies opportunities for improvement and explores the potential for building a modern and resilient control system that responds to present and future challenges.

Main findings

The new preventive control is "exceptional", not binding, and allows risks to be managed in real time. With the creation of the Directorate of Information, Analysis and Immediate Reaction (DIARI), the CGR can monitor, through data analysis, outstanding issues such as the level of execution of infrastructure projects and intervene in a timely manner if they observe cost overruns or delays (real-time surveillance). For example, during the COVID-19 health emergency, the CGR was able to monitor resources in real time by comparing market prices and calculating alleged cost overruns, allowing for timely corrections in public procurement.

However, challenges and opportunities remain. In particular, this study highlights the following:

- There are still concerns associated with the abuses of *ex ante* control in Colombia, eliminated by the 1991 constitutional reform, and with the excessive use of "warnings" during the last decade. Likewise, a collaborative and preventive audit culture is lacking both in the CGR and in the administration. This makes it difficult to take advantage of the new preventive control and undermine its acceptance and ownership.
- There is a high degree of confusion among public officials, both in the CGR and in the public administration, regarding the difference between "alerts" and "warnings" and their relationship with the preventive and concomitant control. Many officials associate preventive control only with alerts. However, the main regulations on preventive control do not refer to "alerts" and it is not clear at what stage an alert can become a warning.
- The excessive formality in issuing "warnings" may be counterproductive for a mechanism that seeks to spur transformation in the public administration through the timely correction of detected issues. In addition, "warnings" can be communicated solely and exclusively by the Comptroller

General. In the future, this could entail a risk of a possible abuse of the new function as well as a risk for the Comptroller General.

- In Colombia, there is no unified, homogenised and open information system in the public sector. This implies that control entities often have their own isolated information systems. The availability and quality of data can vary significantly, thus affecting its use for analytics.

- Preventive control is currently focused on the timely detection of cost overruns and unfinished infrastructure projects. However, there is a lot of potential to make better use of the analytical capacity of the DIARI to strengthen risk management, internal control systems and public administration processes in general.

- There is a need to improve the co-ordination between the Internal Control Units (UCI) and the CGR. In particular, there is concern on the part of the UCI about the scope of their role, the excessive requests for information by the CGR, as well as the feedback on the information they provide. At the same time, there is an opportunity to strengthen and support the work of the UCI with the information generated by the preventive control of the CGR.

- Finally, there is a concern in various sectors of society regarding the continuity of the new mandate over political cycles, in particular given the absence of a public policy of fiscal control that generates a long-term vision and that ensures the institutional continuity of this new way of exercising fiscal control.

Main recommendations

To address the challenges identified, the report provides a series of concrete recommendations to strengthen the use of preventive and concomitant control in Colombia:

- Use the new function of preventive and concomitant control to generate synergies with public entities and thus overcome barriers of mistrust generated by the historic experiences with *ex ante* control.

- Clarify the differentiated use of criteria and the functionality of "alerts" and "warnings", including issuing audit guidelines that broadly outline the practices associated with preventive control.

- Review the process of generating warnings to avoid excessive formality, taking into consideration the need to review the current regulatory framework, as well as the internal processes and procedures for its implementation. In this sense, consider increasing the checks and balances associated with the final decision when issuing a warning.

- Promote a strategy that integrates and leverages the work of the DIARI in relation to preventive and concomitant control within the CGR, including the implementation of data quality models.

- Strengthen the relationship of the CGR with key actors of preventive and concomitant control such as the UCI and promote fluid communication that allows them to use preventive and concomitant control to identify and manage risks within the public administration.

- Promote a long-term vision of fiscal control in Colombia to provide a solid foundation for the continuity of initiatives such as the new preventive and concomitant control mechanism and the related institutional reforms and modernisations promoted in recent years.

1 New preventive and concomitant control in Colombia

This chapter presents the regulatory developments with regard to preventive and concomitant fiscal control in Colombia. It explores its functionalities and opportunities, including the added value that it can give in relation to the identification of risks within public administration. This chapter highlights the importance of continuing to clearly communicate the difference between *ex ante* control and the new preventive and concomitant control as well as to clarify the difference between alerts and warnings.

The context of the new preventive and concomitant control in Colombia

Public governance strategies, driven by the 2007 financial crisis, the economic slowdown and the COVID-19 crisis and its socio-economic consequences, reinforce the need for governments to do more with less and force countries to conduct introspective evaluations of government processes and their results. Moreover, the decrease in citizens' trust in their governments, together with an increase in inequality, particularly in Latin America, underscores the need for public policies to be more efficient, and effective as well as to avoid waste, corruption and fraud in the use of public funds.

Colombia has a sceptical, polarised civil society with low trust in its institutions. For example, the 2021 OECD Government at a Glance reports that only 37% of Colombians expressed trust in the national government, with a 14 percentage point drop in trust compared to 2007 (Figure 1.1).

Figure 1.1. Confidence in national government in 2020 and its change since 2007

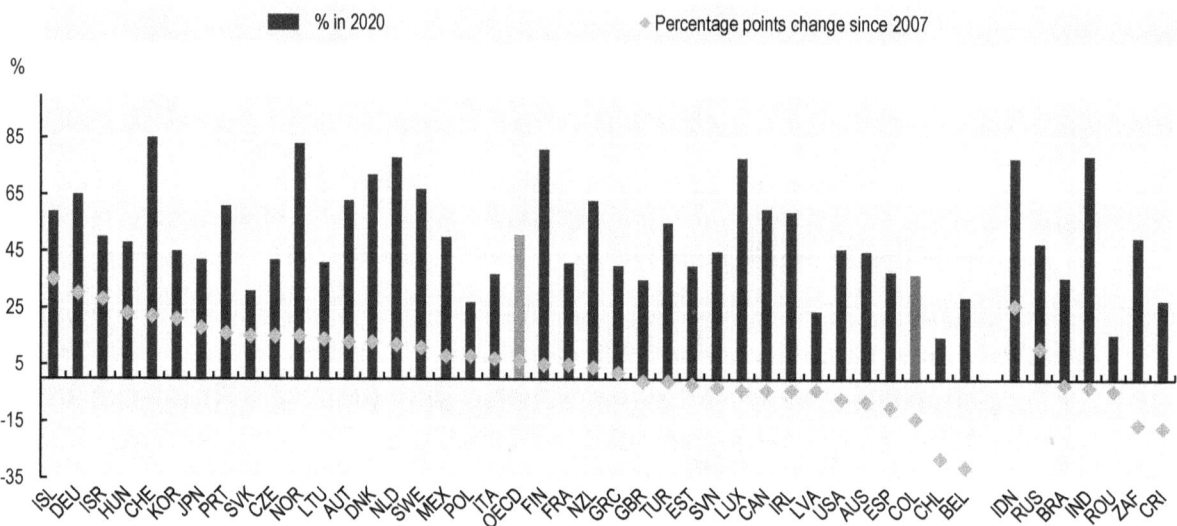

Note: Percentage who answered "yes" to "Do you have confidence in the national government?"
Source: World Gallup Poll, (OECD, 2021[1])

There are several factors that explain trust levels. Undoubtedly, the perception of government integrity is one of the most relevant factors (OECD, 2017[2]; Murtin et al., 2018[3]). As shown in Figure 1.2, citizens in Colombia perceive a high degree of corruption in state institutions that fuels mistrust (OECD, 2018[4]; OECD, 2019[5]; Transparency International, 2019[6]). This mistrust and the perception of corruption, whether based on fact or not, has eroded various aspects of the State-citizen relationship, as well as the relationship between citizens themselves. Aspects such as polarisation and recent cases of corruption in the political class have contributed to this (Observatorio de la Democracia, n.d.[7]). As such, citizens harbour distrust towards legal institutions or the effect that should follow when blowing the whistle. According to the Global Corruption Barometer, 59% of Colombians consider it unlikely that timely action will be taken based on a reported corruption case (Transparency International, 2019[6]) and deem it unlikely that the reporting of an act of corruption will lead to the adoption of strong or appropriate remedial actions (Transparencia por Colombia, 2020[8]).

Figure 1.2. Percentage of people who claim that most or all of the people in these institutions are corrupt in Colombia, 2019

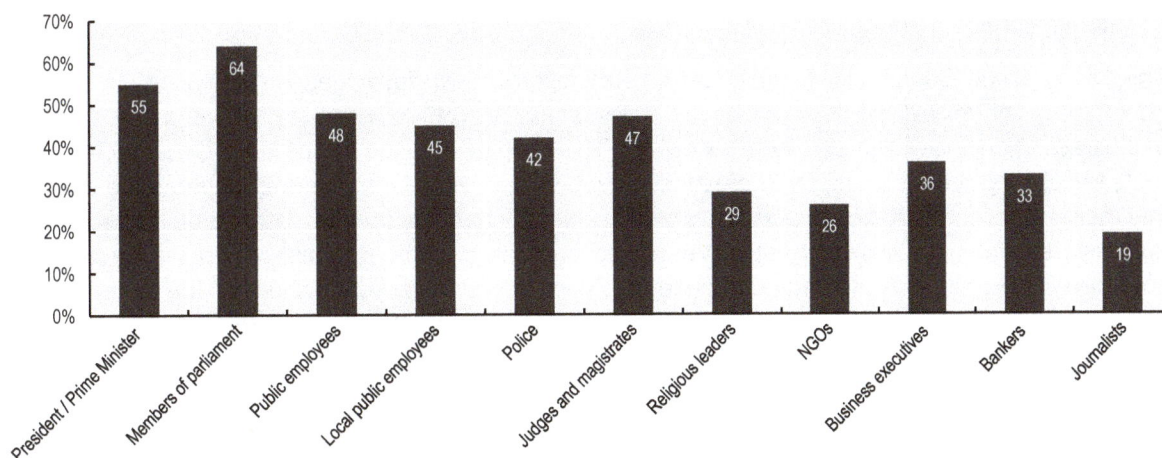

Source: (Transparency International, 2019[6])

To respond to these challenges and an increasingly complex context, it is vital to take steps to restore and build trust in institutions and promote a more systematic understanding of the meaning of effectiveness and efficiency. Supreme Audit Institutions (SAIs) have the potential to help governments meet these challenges and can provide critical evidence of what works and what does not work in public governance, beyond their traditional audit role (OECD, 2016[9]).

In Colombia, the Office of the Comptroller General of the Republic (*Contraloría General de la República*, CGR) is the entity responsible for fiscal oversight and control and is one of the autonomous and independent bodies of the Colombian State. The CGR was created in 1923, then organised as an office for accounting and fiscal control. In 1975, with Law 20, *ex ante* and *ex post* controls were created and the authority of the CGR was expanded to supervise the individuals who manage state assets and resources and endorse public debt contracts. In 1991, fiscal control took a constitutional turn. *Ex ante* control was eliminated and gave way to *ex post* and selective control. Finally, in 2000, the responsibility process was reduced to a single step and the concept of fiscal management and the elements for fiscal responsibility were defined (CGR, 2018[10]). In 2014, in Brasilia, the CGR signed the Declaration of Commitments to the ISSAI Implementation Initiative. In developing this commitment, the principles, foundations and general aspects of the ISSAI standards for financial, compliance and performance audits carried out by the CGR were adopted and guidelines were developed for the three types of audit. New guidelines on territorial audit, complementing the others, was published and updated in 2019.

In the context of the aforementioned challenges and changes within the role of SAIs, a constitutional reform recently granted the CGR a preventive and concomitant control function that allows the identification of risks and red flags while projects and budgets are being executed to allow corrective actions to be taken in real time and in a timely manner. Following international standards, there can be three types of audit at different moments in time (prior, concurrent and subsequent) to generate audit findings with recommendations that go beyond observations made during the audit and allow the closure of identified gaps in public management. Other countries in the region have introduced or are contemplating the introduction of similar reforms (Box 1.1).

Box 1.1. Experience of preventive and concomitant control in Latin America

Concurrent control in Peru

The Office of the Comptroller General of the Republic of Peru developed a new model of external government control with an approach which is essentially preventive, not just punitive, a characteristic of the traditional model of *ex post* external control. This simultaneous control model allows synchronous, multidisciplinary, timely, prompt and preventive support to financial managers throughout the different key moments of the contracting of public goods, services or works, in order to raise alerts about risks and adverse situations identified during the control process, with the purpose of adopting appropriate corrective and preventive measures. Concurrent control reports are published on the Comptroller's website within 72 hours of the report being notified to the competent authorities (Shack Yalta, 2019[11]; Shack, Portugal and Quispe, 2021[12]).

Monitoring (*acompanhamento*) by the Federal Court of Accounts of Brazil

The Federal Court of Accounts of Brazil (*Tribunal de Contas da União*, TCU) sets forth the concomitant and periodic monitoring (*acompanhamento*) of the bodies and entities in its jurisdiction (TCU, 2018[13]). The monitoring consists of audits that are carried out with the main objective of preventing the occurrence of acts that are harmful to the public interest, either because they are in opposition to current regulations or because they do not achieve the planned objectives in an efficient, effective and equitable way. This monitoring is used to examine, over a predetermined period, the legality and legitimacy of the management actions of those subject to TCU's jurisdiction, in accounting, financial, budget and equity matters. It can also be used to evaluate the performance of the bodies and entities under its jurisdiction and of government systems, programmes, projects and activities.

Towards real-time audit in Mexico

In Mexico, a constitutional reform is being considered that provides for audits in real time. They would allow the Audit Office of the Federation (*Auditoría Superior de la Federación*, ASF) to initiate reviews of actions in progress in the audited entities to avoid the occurrence of irregularities. Currently, ASF has already the authority to carry out this type of audit, but they are conditioned on the existence of complaints including supporting documentation. As such, these audits do save time, but are not preventive. The magnitude of the health emergency has evidenced the need for legal powers to carry out real-time audits of public procurement processes. It should be noted that, while the aforementioned constitutional reform is being achieved, the ASF has resorted to a model of preventive or advanced audits through special agreements or protocols while executing their Annual Audit Programme.

Sources: (Shack Yalta, 2019[11]; Shack, Portugal and Quispe, 2021[12]); (TCU, 2018[13]);
https://www.asf.gob.mx/Section/329_F_labor_fiscalizadora.

The advantages and potential of the new preventive and concomitant control by the CGR are significant. The new function is based on the premise of a non-binding, technical approach that does not intend to do more than flag certain situations or events to the audited entity that shed doubts on its performance and that warrant review by the administration itself. For example, the new function allows the CGR to monitor the level of infrastructure project expenses in real time and thus to intervene in a timely manner in case cost overruns or delays are observed without having to wait for the work to be completed and merely document the findings in an *ex post* audit. As such, during the COVID-19 health crisis, the CGR was able to monitor the spending of associated resources in real time. An algorithm was developed to detect the unit cost information from documents pertaining to the contracting processes and compare it to market prices. From there, presumed cost overruns were calculated and corrective actions deployed (Contraloría General de la República de Colombia, 2021[14]).

Furthermore, the new function has the huge potential, yet to be exploited, to prevent mismanagement, fraud and corruption from the outset, through the strengthening of risk management, internal control systems and public administration processes in general. Box 1.2 shows, for example, how audit recommendations have contributed to strengthening internal control in Jamaica.

Box 1.2. The role of SAIs in strengthening internal control in Jamaica: The CARE programme

The audits of internal controls play an important role in preventive and concomitant control due to their great capacity to detect errors and large-scale fraud in real time.

The Jamaican Supreme Audit Institution, for example, conducted three concomitant internal control audits for the information system infrastructure review of the COVID-19 *Allocation of Resources for Employees* (CARE 2020) programme. The Ministry of Finance asked the Auditor General's Department to evaluate whether the internal control system of the support programme for people impacted by COVID-19 is effective in reducing the risk of granting cash payments to ineligible people. Between March and November 2020, the SAI tested the general control and specific controls of CARE's information system and cross-checking of tax administration files and 402 393 applications to determine if they met CARE's eligibility requirements for support.

This audits found that:

- Only 35% of recipients of CARE payments met all the requirements, as of June 2020.
- The information system did not have all necessary controls to ensure the integrity of payments.
- The system reported that payments of USD 5.4 million were withheld from 776 ineligible people, however the Ministry did not produce evidence of such withholding.

Based on the analysis, it was recommended that the ministry improve CARE's specific controls to ensure that only eligible people receive payments and that there is evidence to validate them.

Source: https://auditorgeneral.gov.jm/wp-content/uploads/2020/05/Audit-of-COVID-19-resource-allocation.pdf

---

Furthermore, preventive control can also be of great help in promoting transparency, strengthening accountability and ensuring results. To achieve these objectives, preventive control should not only focus on the identification of shortcomings and findings, but should also allow the accumulation of lessons learned that later can contribute to generate significant changes in the management of public entities and, ultimately, achieve the objectives of public policies and provide efficient and effective public services to citizens.

The objective of this OECD report is to support the CGR in the implementation of this new mandate. It identifies opportunities for its improvement and explores the potential for its preventive use as well as the construction of a national control system in Colombia. The report reviews the efforts carried out since this new faculty was established and analyses the legal and institutional changes for its implementation, including the important role of the Directorate of Information, Analysis and Immediate Reaction (*Dirección de Información, Análisis y Reacción Inmediata*, DIARI). Additionally, it analyses the relationship between preventive control and internal control and risk management in public administration. Finally, the report sets forth recommendations related to the generation and articulation of a fiscal management policy in Colombia to ensure the continuity of preventive control and promote a coherent control system in the country.

The legal framework for preventive and concomitant control in Colombia

The Constitutional reform implemented through Legislative Act 04/2019 has been a decisive step towards preventive and concomitant control in Colombia

In Colombia, preventive and concomitant control is based on the premise of being a function that consists of observing, inspecting and verifying the execution of a programme, project or operation so that the results obtained can be continuously compared with those expected. The different legal instruments related to this new function have made clear that unlike *ex post* control, its function is not to determine observations and findings or initiate fiscal responsibility processes (Figure 1.3). Rather, its role is focused on eliminating potential risks and foreseeable damages. To this extent, it is not intended to pass judgement on the activity of the financial manager ("*gestor fiscal*"), but to prevent damages through an effective mechanism (Corte Constitucional, 2020[15]). Preventive and concomitant control may also perform other functionalities still to be exploited, which will be set out in this report. Among other things, preventive control could contribute to more efficient spending and better management of public finances, or allow more timely and informed risk-related decisions.

Figure 1.3. The legal structure of preventive and concomitant control in Colombia

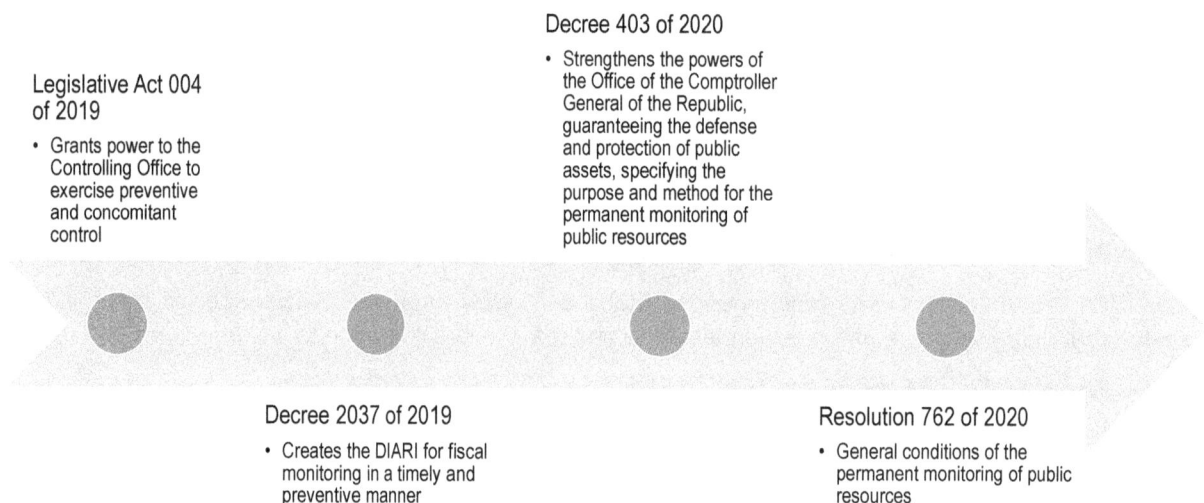

Legislative Act 004 of 2019
- Grants power to the Controlling Office to exercise preventive and concomitant control

Decree 403 of 2020
- Strengthens the powers of the Office of the Comptroller General of the Republic, guaranteeing the defense and protection of public assets, specifying the purpose and method for the permanent monitoring of public resources

Decree 2037 of 2019
- Creates the DIARI for fiscal monitoring in a timely and preventive manner

Resolution 762 of 2020
- General conditions of the permanent monitoring of public resources

Source: (Contraloría General de la República de Colombia, 2021[14])

Legislative Act 04 of 2019 amends articles 267, 268, 271, 272 and 274 of the Political Constitution to strengthen the constitutional and legal regime of fiscal oversight and control, incorporating, among others, article 267 on constitutional concomitant and preventive control, exclusive to the Office of the Comptroller General of the Republic, to complement *ex post* and selective control to guarantee the defence and protection of public goods. Concomitant and preventive control does not imply co-administration, it is of an "exceptional" nature and will be carried out in real time through permanent monitoring, thus allowing the audit function to be implemented in real time "through the use of information technologies, with the active participation of public oversight and the articulation with internal control". The reform establishes the function of the CGR to warn public servants and individuals who manage public resources of the existence of imminent risks in operations or processes. It attributes the issuance of such "warnings" (*advertencias*) to the exclusive remit of the person of the Comptroller General (Gomez Lee, 2020[16]). The reform also allows the control of fiscal management to be carried out at all administrative levels and with respect to all types of public resources, including not only national but also territorial entities.

In turn, Constitutional Court ruling C-140/20 has warned about the limits of this new function. In this sense, preventive and concomitant control cannot influence management decisions to the point of instituting a system of co-administration or co-management, which is expressly prohibited by constitutional amendment. It also establishes that the concept of "warning" should allow not only the identification of the risks which loom over some projects, but should also give financial managers and executives the opportunity to carry out corrective actions prior to the generation of damages. Finally, it determines that the General Warning System (*Sistema General de Advertencias*, where the warnings issued by the CGR are recorded) must be used only for the purpose of preventing damages and, furthermore, to exercise control over risks and not over particular actions.

Working with entities to overcome barriers of mistrust generated by ex ante *control and improving communication and interaction around preventive and concomitant control*

The Constitutional Court has emphasised that the new preventive control is not *ex ante* control such as the one that was eliminated in Colombia via the 1991 Political Constitution. At that time, the National Constituent Assembly decided to exclude the concept of *ex ante* control as it was considered ineffective and harmful, given that, according to the social imaginary, it had become an arbitrary co-administration system (González Zapata and Mosquera Perea, 2019[17]). According to the report of the fifth commission of public finance and the budget of the constituent authority:

> *"...ex ante control, standard in Colombia, has been disastrous for the public administration because it has distorted the objective of the Office of the Comptroller General by allowing it to abuse a certain co-administration, resulting in the comptroller having vast unipersonal power and has also lent itself to a cumbersome bureaucratic process that degenerates into corruption."*

However, since the constitutional change, academics and control entities have been vocal about the imminent need to establish more preventive tools and the possibility of identifying damages to public assets before they materialise (PGN, 2012[18]) (Uprimny Yepes and Sánchez Duque, 2012[19]) (Avellaneda y Asociados, 2019[20]). The constitutional reform set forth in Legislative Act 4 of 2019 was established based on this logic.

During the interviews carried out within the framework of this project, it became clear that there is a high level of concern or confusion among the public administration and the CGR regarding the differences between preventive and *ex ante* control. As such, it was evident that the perceptions that continue to affect the relationship between public entities and the CGR, as well as fears related to co-administration, still exist.

Although the historical reasons that led to a profound rejection of *ex ante* control are understandable, the concept of a preventive control is very different. The new norm does not affect the principle of separation of powers, it precisely establishes the limits, precautions and prohibitions under which the new preventive and concomitant control must be exercised (Corte Constitucional, 2020[15]). In this context, the new powers that were attributed to the Comptroller General are not absolute powers. On the contrary, far from usurping and replacing public powers, they have precise limits and are part of the competencies that exist in other American countries and that are common practice in other regions (Gomez Lee, 2020[16]).

Indeed, according to the reform, the new preventive and concomitant fiscal control model must comprise five main characteristics:

- It must not involve co-administration, it will be carried out in real time through permanent monitoring of cycles, use, execution, contracting and impact of public resources, using information technologies and with the active involvement of social control and the support of internal control.
- It is exceptional and non-binding.
- It does not dictate on the advisability of the decisions of the administrators of public resources.
- It will be implemented in the form of a "warning" to the financial manager.
- Its implementation and co-ordination will fall exclusively to the Comptroller General of the Republic in specific matters.

Undoubtedly, preventive and concomitant control is a useful tool to ensure timely fiscal control and is a valuable instrument in the fight against corruption. That is why its use must be enshrined within the framework of the restrictions of Legislative Act 04 of 2019. As such, the investment of time and resources into its implementation must be ensured, including adequate communication strategies that generate trust between public institutions, citizens and other stakeholders. All of this is needed to reinforce the understanding of the existing legal framework and to allow entities to understand that this reform is a platform to improve their processes and of the control systems. As such, even when the decision making of public servants is based on their discretion and the framework of the regulations that regulates their competences, they must also consider compliance with the mission objectives of their function. In this framework, a SAI alerting of a risk should not override that ability but rather constitute a parameter to be taken into account with seriousness and due care in the final decision making of the public servants.

To this end, the CGR could consider, firstly, reinforcing knowledge and understanding of the concept of preventive and concomitant control, making a clear distinction from the concept of *ex ante control. This could be achieved through the promotion of the new function to generate trust in public* or private institutions that administer public resources. As such, to avoid confusion related to *ex ante* control, it is necessary to continue proactively communicating the particularities of preventive control and to make available a guide or jurisprudential line that outlines the practices associated with preventive control, including examples of which actions actually constitute *ex ante* control and may constitute co-administration and which actions are typical of preventive and concomitant control. This undertaking could contrast these practices with the current regulatory framework, aiming at further strengthening the control and surveillance of public resources and the transformation of the rules that regulate it (Torres Calderón and Montes Arrieta, 2020[21]).

Secondly, the CGR could promote a cultural change to allow the effective implementation of the new preventive and concomitant control. The legal reform is only the first step in a transformation process related to fiscal control. To achieve this transformation, it is necessary to work on promoting cultural change both within the Comptroller's Office (Chapter 2) and also within other state entities (Chapters 3 and 4). Promoting such change is an incremental process that requires efforts at different levels. Various aspects will be covered in the following chapters. However, it is worth emphasising here that in addition to communication efforts, discussions should be held within the CGR and with its Departmental Management Offices (*Gerencias Departamentales Colegiadas*) with regard to the different roles fulfilled by the CGR, including on preventive and concomitant control.

Thirdly, opening of a dialogue at the state level in Colombia could be considered to analyse the possibility to enable the CGR to provide constructive recommendations to public administrations on how to address and mitigate the risks or problems identified in audits or during preventive control. At the moment, ruling C-103 of 2015 of the Constitutional Court establishes the prohibition of issuing recommendations for *ex post* control, considering them as co-administration. However, according to the international practice of SAIs and ISSAI 100, formulating constructive recommendations to take corrective actions is part of the

Fundamental Principles of Public Sector Auditing (INTOSAI, 2019[22]). Making recommendations is not co-administration as long as the auditor is careful not to assume management responsibilities, particularly in relation to defining public policy objectives, for example. Aiming at increasing the value and benefit of SAIs, the International Organization of Supreme Audit Institutions (INTOSAI), in guideline P-12 of its third principle, seeks to:

- "identify themes, common outcomes, links, root causes and audit recommendations; and discuss them with key stakeholders";
- "without compromising its independence, provide advice on how the results and opinions of its audits should be used, so that they have a greater impact; for example, through the provision of advice on good practice";
- "report as appropriate on subsequent action to be taken following their recommendations" (INTOSAI, 2019[23]).

Thus, such recommendations could be of great use to the operators of fiscal control and to the public administration and could help promoting a more positive and constructive relationship between the CGR and the administration. This function operates on a recurring basis in other countries, where SAIs provide feedback and recommendations to the public administration based on their audit findings and thus contribute to improving public management by offering possible avenues for corrective actions and risk mitigation. EUROSAI recently published a report on good practice in following up on audit recommendations which could inspire and inform changes in Colombia (EUROSAI, 2021[24]).

Finally, it is crucial to assertively measure the achievements and results of the preventive and concomitant control of the CGR. In particular, the detection and opening of cases should not be the main indicator for its effectiveness. While it is important to show short-term results that reflect the number of public resources recovered, it is recommended to move towards the use of indicators that measure impacts and results related to effective service delivery and structural changes in the public administration. Such changes can not only help mitigate future risks, but can also provide an estimation of public resources saved thanks to preventive and concomitant control and/or the negative consequences that could arise without its existence. For example, through the analysis of the risks detected, SAIs can develop and communicate "macro control reports" in which, in an aggregate and systematic way, they can warn about the need for changes in public management processes, which include reviews of the processes aimed at improving the performance of public entities. In other words, showing the advantages of taking risks into account in a timelier manner also helps to prevent them from materialising.

Indeed, the evolution of the role of SAIs in promoting good governance has led to a diversification of their strategic objectives, their audits and their advisory role to include the delivery of evidence-based information and insight into public policy decision making, as a complement to traditional supervisory activities (OECD, 2016[9]). Performance audits or data-driven dashboards that track or predict economic changes are just a few examples of these activities.

Thus, the impact of a SAIs in terms of relevant results could be measured, for example, in terms of:

- Estimates of savings made due to the measures implemented.
- Increases in revenue.
- Reductions in costs.
- Increased satisfaction with the provision of public services provided by the public administration.
- The provision of legal security by guaranteeing compliance with legal frameworks.
- Improvements in the achievement of other policy objectives, e.g. related to the SDGs (environmental quality, education, health, gender equality, fight against corruption and integrity, etc.).

Preventive and concomitant control through "alerts" and "warnings"

Preventive and concomitant control is carried out through "warnings" and "alerts"

One of the most important characteristics of preventive and concomitant control is the way in which it is implemented in theory and in practice. Legislative Act 4 of 2019, Art. 267 refers to its implementation only "in the form of a warning to the financial manager". As such, Decree 403 of 2020 develops the provisions of articles 267 and 268 of the Political Constitution for the strengthening of fiscal control. Article 67 of said Decree also states that the conducting of preventive and concomitant control shall be manifested through the issuance of "warnings" by the Comptroller General of the Republic. This warning relates to the event or risk identified and is based on monitoring exercises and the permanent monitoring of public resources. Whenever the event or risk may impact more than one entity or object of control, a "general warning" may be issued.

In turn, through Art. 56 of Resolution 762 of 2020, the general conditions of "the permanent monitoring of public resources" and the conditions for the implementation of preventive and concomitant control were developed. In this document, the scope of preventive and concomitant control was expanded, rendering the process of permanent monitoring of public resources as an early alert and as a prior step to the "warnings". This activity consists of identifying (with the support of the Internal Control Units (*Unidades de Control Interno*, UCI) of the public administration and social control, among others) early alerts as information for control exercises. The following sections describe these two concepts of "warnings" and "alerts" and analyse them in more detail.

The "warning" mechanism

The concept of "warning" is not new to the CGR. On the contrary, it is set forth in the reform of Law Decree 267 of 2000 (Art. 5) establishing the function of warnings for operations or processes being implemented to prevent serious risks that could compromise public assets and exercise *ex post* control over the events identified. On several occasions, particularly during the 2013-2015 period, the CGR had used tools with similar functionalities to those of preventive and concomitant control. In particular, reports were prepared that highlighted the enormous fiscal risks to public assets of some government operations. Warning mechanisms were used in these reports, such as the one carried out in the case of the sale of Telecom to Telmex and of the Ministry of Mining regarding the exploitation of gas in La Guajira (CGR, 2012-2014[25]).

Said provision was in force for more than 15 years until the Constitutional Court declared it at odds with the limits established for fiscal control in 2015, given that the figure was the subject of arduous debates about its role, in particular co-administration and its aforementioned overuse. According to the Constitutional Court, the warning constituted a modality of *ex ante* control and, in the words of the Court, contained the "capacity to influence the decisions and the course of the processes and operations of the administrative authorities subject to surveillance, insofar as the course of actions can be transformed" (Corte Constitucional, 2015[26]). This could be understood as favourable as it can prevent any detriment to public assets, but it could, in turn, affect the independence of *ex post* audits to be carried out because these could be flawed due the previous intervention made. Thus, the CGR's warning mechanism was incorporated into the internal control system, which was called upon to generate the appropriate mechanisms to ensure fiscal management to be efficient, equitable and effective or that it takes into account the assessment of environmental costs (González Zapata and Mosquera Perea, 2019[17]).

For this reason, the 2019 reform brings back the mechanism, adding the checks and balances mentioned in the previous section, including conceptual clarity related to its exceptional nature and the explicit prohibition of co-administration. Thus a "warning", as established in article 68 of the aforementioned Decree and Resolution 762 of 2020, Art. 32, is a non-binding statement by which the Comptroller General of the Republic warns a financial manager about the detection of an imminent risk of loss of public resources and/or a negative impact on public assets or interests, so that the financial manager can autonomously evaluate the adoption of measures deemed appropriate to exercise control over the events and prevent damages from materialising or spreading.

As such, Art. 69 of Decree 403 of 2020 establishes the methodology and a criterion of necessity according to the analysis of the following specific matters to which is pertains: a) social significance; b) high environmental impact; and c) high economic connotation.

In turn, the applicable phases Art.34 of Resolution 762 of 2020 are as follows:

- **Planning phase**, determining the follow-up activities to be carried out, the implementation milestones thereof, the objectives, expected results, success criteria and the risks of the process in question.
- **Implementation phase**, the application of procedures to obtain pertinent information, analysis thereof and determining the foreseeable results and the effectiveness of the controls with regard to risks identified or unforeseen adverse situations.
- **Internal reporting phase**, where the selected management milestones, risks identified, working documents and media, as well as conclusions and recommendations are presented to the legal office in order to be submitted for consideration by the Comptroller General.

This Resolution specifies the step-by-step process for generating warnings (Figure 1.4) and stipulates that, based on the aforementioned internal report to the Legal Office, the warning issued shall include the legal basis, a succinct exposition of the facts and the identification of the imminent risk of loss of public resources and/or negative impacts on public assets or interests.

Figure 1.4. Procedure for the generation of "warnings"

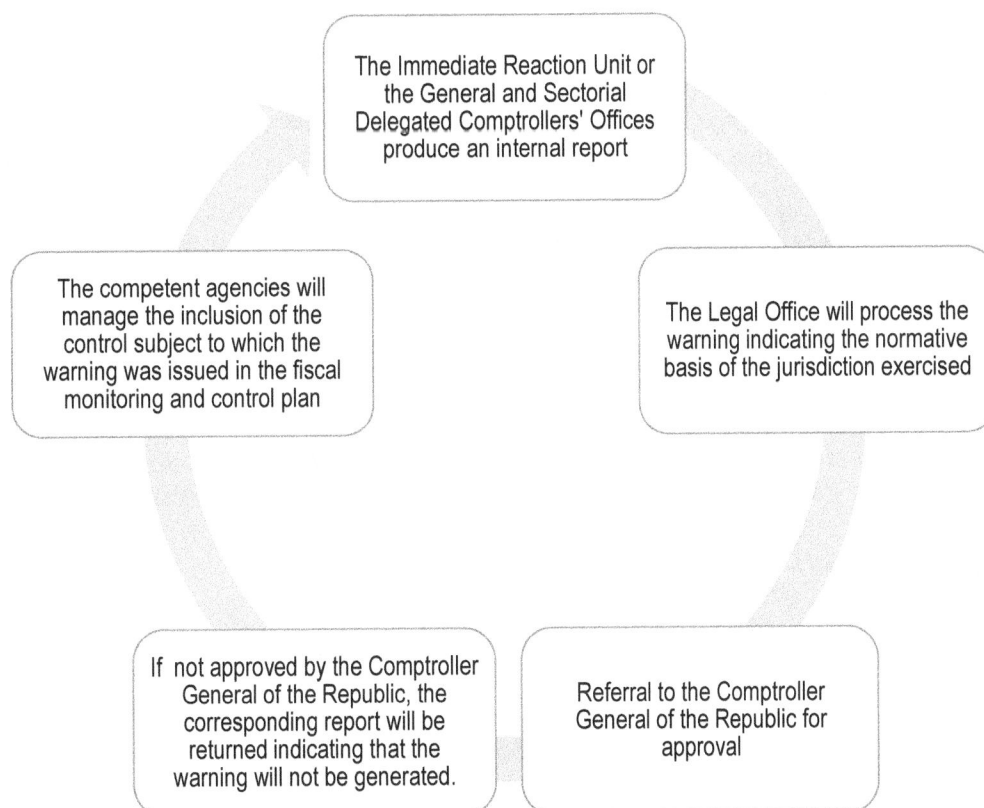

Source: (CGR, 2020[27])

The "alert" mechanism (permanent monitoring of public resources)

The vast majority of stakeholders interviewed for this study related preventive and concomitant control to the "early alerts" issued by the CGR over the last year. Art. 4 of Resolution 762 of 2020 states that the Directorate of Information, Analysis and Immediate Reaction *(Direccion de Información, Analisis y Reacción Inmediata, DIARI)* and the General and Sectorial Delegated Comptrollers' Offices *(Contralores Delegados Generales y Sectoriales)* will be able to generate and send early alerts to the corresponding dependencies of the CGR, territorial comptrollers, other competent public authorities and citizens for the purpose of promoting social control interventions.

Early alerts are understood as a "brief and succinct reports of the preliminary detection of any possible risks of affectation or loss of public resources, which serve as an input to the exercise of fiscal control and do not constitute warnings to the fiscal manager". In this sense, the alert can come from social participatory forums, from exchanges with internal control or from other sources, such as the data analytics work carried out by the DIARI. Early alerts are established on the basis of the collection and analysis of information on financial management in all its stages and cycles, as well as the development or execution of the processes or decision making of control subjects, without intervening therein or causing interference. This allows to obtain useful information to monitor and analyse the risks and controls associated with the planning, use, execution, contracting and impact of public goods, funds or resources and to carry out the preventive and concomitant or *ex post* fiscal control.

According to the interviews conducted for this study, the "early alerts" target various stakeholders. First, they are redirected for the purposes of social control to working groups with entities and citizens. Second, they are sent to other control entities (territorial comptrollers, prosecutor's office, attorney's office, superintendencies) for the purpose of investigating the facts presented and finally they are shared with other dependencies of the CGR for the purpose of contributing to other fiscal management exercises with the same alerted entity (audits, improvement plans).

Even though, from the executive branch, different tools with similar objectives have existed throughout history in Colombia, none had allowed for an institutionalisation of this permanent monitoring. An example of this are the Visible Audits *(Auditorías Visibles)* and Democracy Watch *(Vigías de la Democracia)* programmes in departments and municipalities and the "White Elephants" application developed by the National Government's Transparency Secretariat.

- The Visible Audits and Democracy Watch programmes, in which citizens actively participated, were designed by the National Government to control the use of resources in the departments and municipalities that receive royalties derived from crude oil. These tools sought to ensure that public infrastructure projects were executed in accordance with the provisions of the contract for each project and to avoid irregularities in their execution and construction processes (DNP, 2021[28]).

- In 2014, the National Government's Transparency Secretariat launched the application for the identification and georeferencing of "white elephants." In this case, it sought to identify and monitor public works whose construction was halted or abandoned. With the application, users could take photographs of unfinished public works and enter information about the entities responsible for them, which could be completed by different people. This was followed by a kind of "alert" from the Transparency Secretariat to the contracting entity about the inappropriate use of resources and the possibility of generating a plan for their correction.

However, these tools have been disappearing, leaving an institutional vacuum in relation to the generation of alerts on the mismanagement of public resources in real time. As a result, the preventive and concomitant control of the CGR represents an opportunity not only to institutionalise a set of good practices and initiatives already developing albeit haphazardly, but to add high-quality technical and technological elements, making use of specialised human resources and multidisciplinary teams that use technology intensively (photogrammetry, drones and georeferencing, among others) to obtain appropriate and sufficient evidence for appropriate interventions.

Even though warnings and alerts are important preventive and concomitant control tools, the CGR should work to clarify their functionality and the differentiated use of criteria for each one

As mentioned above, the new powers of the CGR seek more preventive action as it relates to the sources and uses of public resources, intervening long before the damage to public assets has materialised and is irreversible (DNP, 2021[29]). However, adjustments to the practical use of this new control are necessary to ensure its success.

First and as evidenced throughout the interviews conducted for this study, there is confusion among public officials, both from the CGR and from State entities, regarding the "alert" and "warning" mechanisms and its relationship with preventive and concomitant control. In particular, it became clear that the majority of those interviewed, at the national and territorial level, had seen and were aware of preventive control solely and exclusively through the use of alerts; an example of this were the interviews at the territorial level where there was no knowledge of the role of warnings in preventive and concomitant control or even the role of DIARI in generating alerts.

Part of this confusion may be due to the regulatory dispersion related to preventive and concomitant control, which contains regulatory provisions in various sources (Legislative Act, Decree, Resolution and Executive Regulatory Resolution). As such, the fact that the main regulatory bodies of preventive and concomitant control do not refer to "alerts" (Legislative Act 4 of 2019 or Decree 403 of 2020) may contribute to the misperception. An example of this was the misunderstanding that the public administration identified in the remit of the Sectorial Delegate Comptrollers to issue alerts, since giving its confusion with the warnings, would be of absolute competence of the Comptroller General. However the two occur at different times and fulfil different functionalities. This is why explaining and teaching about the particularities of each one will contribute to changing the perception of third parties with regard thereto, in particular to recognise that the mechanism has the potential to go beyond a follow-up of unfinished works or "white elephants".

Second, the interviews revealed problems within procedural aspects. In particular, there is an internal and external misunderstanding regarding the processes and procedures applicable to each functionality. To better understand the operation of preventive and concomitant control, it is necessary to refer to Decree 403 of 2020 (Art. 58) and Resolution 762 of 2020, which establish procedures for the generation of "alerts" and "warnings". In the fiscal surveillance macro process VIG 01 PR 001 there is a clear differentiation between the criteria and processes for alerts and warnings, helping to clarify the indiscriminate references to "concomitant and preventive control" or to the "permanent monitoring of public resources" within the legislation. However, in the interviews conducted for this study, most of the relevant stakeholders were unaware of this macro process and even the particularities of the legislation. For this reason, reinforcements are required through training activities to provide clarity on the entire chain of actors involved in preventive control within the CGR, including aspects related to its practical implementation. An example of this problem was the aforementioned general lack of clarity about which stage determines when an alert can become a warning or even the role of such relevant actors as the DIARI, which the vast majority of actors in the territory were unaware had a role in preventive and concomitant control. As such, experts consulted for this study highlighted a fundamental issue related to the lack of criteria in the evaluation when converting "alert" reports to "warning" reports, signed by the Comptroller.

Third, in procedural terms, an additional issue merits attention and is related to the final decision-making role, which falls solely and exclusively to the Comptroller General. Several interviews conducted for this study highlighted the need to find a mechanism that prevents the final decision from falling exclusively to one person, avoiding the risk of possible abuses of the mechanism in the future, as well as the risk incurred by whoever holds the position of Comptroller General. This internal deliberation process on the use of the warnings could benefit from the use of a sort of technical committee to support the final decision of the Comptroller General or the publication of minutes on the meetings that led to the final decision. In this vein, objective criteria could perhaps be established or the rationale be more documented regarding the application of a warning. As explained before, these measures could protect decision makers, protect the mechanism from being used with political motives in the future and afford additional legitimacy towards external actors.

Finally, even though these two functions have great potential, there is still no clarity on how alerts or warnings could serve to provide feedback and leveraging processes in public administration, like, for example, in Spain where there is a model that allows the identification of risk factors through automated reviews carried out in conjunction with the public administration (Box 1.3). Unfortunately, in Colombia the limits and formalities of both figures have contributed little to interrelations with the public administration, which according to interviews conducted by the OECD, continue to see this tool as a form of control, rather than a way of identifying and correcting risks in a preventive manner.

Box 1.3. Assessing risks in the continuous monitoring system in Spain

Risk factors

Directive HFP / 371/2018 provides the basis for how the National Audit Office (ONA) ultimately defines and interprets risk in the context of its ongoing supervisory role. The Directive requires three levels of verification for ONA to assess public organisations for compliance, financial sustainability and relevance. Together, these risk factors form the basis of the concept of "rationality of structures" of public organisations, as defined in the Directive. Through this "rationality" lens, ONA interprets risk and shapes its automated reviews and ongoing monitoring methodology. As defined by law, ongoing monitoring is not explicitly intended to identify a broader set of strategic, operational or reputational risks, including fraud or corruption risks, if they fall outside the scope of the concept of rationality.

Automated reviews

"Automated" reviews are risk assessments that the ONA performs based on indicators derived from financial and economic data reported by public sector organisations to the IGAE, as well as other qualitative information. Reviews are "automatic" in the sense that data is collected and indicators are generated in an Excel spreadsheet using formulas. Automated reviews apply to all of the aforementioned organisations that are under the scope of continuous monitoring. ONA collaborated with the Office of Finance and Information Technology (OIP) within the IGAE in the design of the tool that automatically generates financial and economic indicators and ratios. The end result of the automated reviews is called the Automated Actions Report, which communicates the results of the risk analysis.

Source: Interpretation of the Official Gazette of the Government of Spain (Government of Spain, 2018[30])

Thus, preventive and concomitant control, by way of the "alerts" generated through the DIARI and Sectorial Delegate Comptrollers, in its link to internal control, could be more focused on supporting risk management within the public administration and even allow entities to reschedule their audit plans based on these risks. An example of this was evidenced in the interviews conducted for this study, where Medellin's Mayor's Office deemed the given alert very useful for the reprogramming of its Annual Audit Plan. Another example of the potential of the mechanism is the predictive pre-contractual and contractual risk model for monitoring State contracting that is conducted via the classification of contracts based on key concepts, integration of sources, data preparation, calculation of risk levels and visualisations (Contraloría General de la República de Colombia, 2021[14]). This predictive model would have the potential to leverage improvements in the management of public administration.

In this regard, the CGR could consider the following recommendations:

- Disseminate and train on the existing legal framework, including the internal regulations of the CGR related to the processes and procedures associated with alerts and warnings, emphasising the differences and functionalities of each one. The CGR could even consider the unification of normative instruments (Decrees, Resolutions and Executive Regulatory Resolutions) into a single regulatory framework and the unification of terms and concepts (e.g. the difference between early warnings issued by the CGR and early warnings issued by internal control) that help clarify the role and functionalities of the different stages of the process.

- Generate an audit guide or an illustrative booklet aimed at entities, Departmental Management Offices and dependencies of the CGR where the operation of the two mechanisms and the actors that intervene in each one are explained, through examples and case studies. This would be a great opportunity to highlight the difference between the warning and alert processes and the differentiated objectives with *ex post* control. This guide will also make it possible to highlight the role of the DIARI in the process and help to generate appropriate channels of communication between the different areas of the CGR. The guide or booklet could also serve to make more strategic use of preventive control, concentrating on the task of identifying risks and not only serving as an instrument for detecting problems in a timelier manner. In this way, it could be used to leverage the processes of identification, management and feedback, for the risks identified in the public administration and thereof contribute to the planning and execution stages of internal audits or even, through an analysis of historical information, identify recurring problems in the planning and execution of public resources.

- Consider establishing checks and balances in the decision-making process with regards to the warning function. In particular, analyse the possibility of including supporting documents or a synthesis of the decision-making process in the publication of the warning, as well as a forum for internal deliberation within the CGR that supports the final decision issued by the Comptroller General.

References

Avellaneda y Asociados (2019), *Entrevista: Colombia necesita un Código de control y responsabilidad fiscal*, Ambito Juridico, https://avellanedaayasociados.com/colombia-necesita-un-codigo-de-control-y-responsabilidad-fiscal (accessed on 10 September 2021). [20]

CGR (2020), *Resolucion 762/2020*. [27]

CGR (2018), *Historia y Contralores - Contraloría General de la República*, https://www.contraloria.gov.co/contraloria/la-entidad/historia-y-contralores (accessed on 6 September 2021). [10]

CGR (2012-2014), *Funciones de Advertencia - Política de tratamiento de datos personales - Contraloría General de la República*, https://www.contraloria.gov.co/politica-de-tratamiento-de-datos-personales/ (accessed on 27 October 2021). [25]

Contraloría General de la República de Colombia (2021), *Una Contraloría para Todos: informe de Gestión 2020-2021*. [14]

Corte Constitucional (2020), *C-140-20 Corte Constitucional de Colombia*, https://www.corteconstitucional.gov.co/relatoria/2020/C-140-20.htm (accessed on 19 July 2021). [15]

Corte Constitucional (2015), *C-103-15 Corte Constitucional de Colombia*, https://www.corteconstitucional.gov.co/RELATORIA/2015/C-103-15.htm (accessed on 5 November 2021). [26]

DNP (2021), *Auditores Ciudadanos*, https://auditoresciudadanos.dnp.gov.co. [28]

DNP (2021), *CONPES 4045*, https://colaboracion.dnp.gov.co/CDT/Conpes/Econ%C3%B3micos/4045.pdf (accessed on 8 September 2021). [29]

EUROSAI (2021), *Follow-up of the implementation of audit recommendations: Best practices guide, issued by the project group*, European Organisation of Supreme Audit Institutions (EUROSAI). [24]

Gomez Lee, I. (2020), *El control fiscal concomitante y de advertencia | Ámbito Jurídico*, Ambito Juridico, https://www.ambitojuridico.com/noticias/analisis/administrativo-y-contratacion/el-control-fiscal-concomitante-y-de-advertencia (accessed on 19 July 2021). [16]

González Zapata, A. and L. Mosquera Perea (2019), "Del control previo y perceptivo al posterior y preventivo: estudio de la trayectoria en el control fiscal en Colombia (1991-2019)". [17]

Government of Spain (2018), *Official Gazette (Boletín Oficial del Estado),*, https://www.boe.es/eli/es/o/2018/04/09/hfp371. [30]

INTOSAI (2019), *INTOSAI-P 12 The Value and Benefits of Supreme Audit Institutions: Making a difference to the lives of citizens*, AuditInternational Organisation of Supreme Audit Institutions (INTOSAI). [23]

INTOSAI (2019), *ISSAI 100 Fundamental Principles of Public-Sector Auditing*, International Organisation of Supreme Audit Institutions (INTOSAI), https://www.issai.org/pronouncements/issai-100-fundamental-principles-of-public-sector-auditing/ (accessed on 17 May 2021). [22]

Murtin, F. et al. (2018), "Trust and its determinants: Evidence from the Trustlab experiment", *OECD Statistics Working Papers*, No. 2, https://doi.org/10.1787/869ef2ec-en. [3]

Observatorio de la Democracia (n.d.), *De qué va la polarización en Colombia*, 2019, https://obsdemocracia.org/2019/05/21/de-que-va-la-polarizacion-en-colombia/ (accessed on 6 September 2021). [7]

OECD (2021), *Government at a Glance 2021*, OECD Publishing, Paris, http://dx.doi.org/10.1787/1c258f55-en. [1]

OECD (2019), *La Integridad Pública en América Latina y el Caribe 2018-2019: De Gobiernos reactivos a Estados proactivos*, OECD, Paris, https://www.oecd.org/gov/integridad/integridad-publica-en-america-latina-caribe-2018-2019.htm. [5]

OECD (2018), *Integrity for Good Governance in Latin America and the Caribbean: From Commitments to Action*, OECD Publishing, Paris, https://dx.doi.org/10.1787/9789264201866-en. [4]

OECD (2017), *Trust and Public Policy: How Better Governance Can Help Rebuild Public Trust*, OECD Public Governance Reviews, OECD Publishing, Paris, https://dx.doi.org/10.1787/9789264268920-en. [2]

OECD (2016), *Supreme Audit Institutions and Good Governance: Oversight, Insight and Foresight*, OECD Public Governance Reviews, OECD Publishing, Paris, https://dx.doi.org/10.1787/9789264263871-en. [9]

PGN (2012), "Modelo de Gestión de la Función Preventiva de la Procuraduría General de la Nación". [18]

Shack Yalta, N. (2019), *Modelo de Control Concurrente como eje central de un enfoque preventivo, célere y oportuno del Control Gubernamental en el Perú*, Contraloría General de la República del Perú, Lima. [11]

Shack, N., L. Portugal and R. Quispe (2021), "El Control Concurrente: Estimando cuantitativamente sus beneecios NELSON SHACK LUIS PORTUGAL RICHAR QUISPE", *Documento de Política en Control Gubernamental*, Contraloría General de la República del Perú, Lima, https://doc.contraloria.gob.pe/estudios-especiales/documento_trabajo/2021/Paper_Control_Concurrente_2021_9JUL2021.pdf (accessed on 10 September 2021). [12]

TCU (2018), *Manual Acompanhamento TCU*, https://portal.tcu.gov.br/data/files/BC/B4/76/F4/A4A1F6107AD96FE6F18818A8/Manual_acompanhamento.pdf. [13]

Torres Calderón, J. and M. Montes Arrieta (2020), *Normas constitucionales y legales del control fiscal en el marco de la evaluación integral de las contralorías territoriales*, http://dx.doi.org/10.15332/dt.inv.2020.01098. [21]

Transparencia por Colombia (2020), *La denuncia de la corrupción y la protección al denunciante en Colombia*, http://www.transparenciacolombia.org.co (accessed on 6 September 2021). [8]

Transparency International (2019), *Global Corruption Barometer - Latin America*, https://www.transparency.org/en/gcb/latin-america/latin-america-and-the-caribbean-x-edition-2019 (accessed on 6 September 2021). [6]

Uprimny Yepes, R. and L. Sánchez Duque (2012), "Constitución de 1991, justicia constitucional y cambio democrático: un balance dos décadas después", *http://journals.openedition.org/cal* 71, pp. 33-53, http://dx.doi.org/10.4000/CAL.2663. [19]

2 Strengthening the Office of the Comptroller General for implementing preventive and concomitant control in Colombia

This chapter presents the opportunities and challenges of the implementation of the new preventive and concomitant control, particularly in relation to its internal governance, the role played by the different dependencies of the Office of the Comptroller General and the cultural change needed for the development of this new tool. In particular, it highlights the challenges of internal co-ordination, data use and analytics as well as opportunities to leverage processes such as performance audits and sectorial studies.

From theory to practice: challenges in the internal governance of preventive and concomitant control in the CGR and recommendations for its institutionalisation and appropriation

There are no regulatory reforms which, alone, respond to all of the issues related to the implementation of a new project or mechanism. In essence, the institutional arrangements associated with any regulatory reform are perhaps equally or even more important to its success than the regulatory reform itself. For this reason, this chapter focuses on the successes and opportunities of the current arrangements and practices, as well as the imperative need for the appropriation of the mechanism and its various elements by CGR officials.

The legal changes to the reform introduced by Legislative Act 04 of 2019 and the new approach to preventive and concomitant control required adjustments to the internal institutional framework of the CGR. The CGR is divided into different dependencies. Among them, the Sectorial Delegate Comptrollers (*Contralorías Delegadas Sectoriales*) with macro and micro areas and the General Delegate Comptrollers (*Contralorias Delegadas Generales*), as well as the units and support offices (such as the DIARI or the Legal Office) and the Departmental Management Offices.

- The CGR has four General Delegate Comptrollers (Figure 2.1). Under the preventive and concomitant control, the Delegate for Citizen Participation intervenes in relation to the observations of the citizens and the administration of the Internal Control Early Warning System (*Sistema de Alertas de Control Interno, SACI*).

Figure 2.1. General Delegate Comptrollers

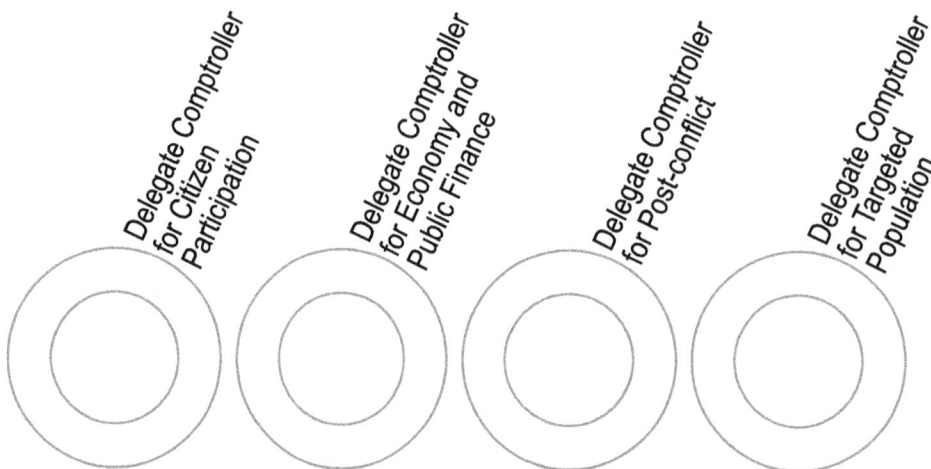

- In addition, in accordance with Law 267 of 2000, the Sectorial Delegate Comptrollers have two directorates: one for fiscal surveillance, whose function is to direct the implementation of policies, plans, programmes and projects related to micro fiscal surveillance and control. Equally, they have a macro fiscal control area, which includes a Direction for Sectorial Studies in charge of analysing policies, plans and programmes in the respective sector. Today there are 11 Sectorial Delegate Comptrollers Offices Table 2.1, who carry out special audits or investigations related to events of national impact that require the immediate intervention of the entity, due to the imminent risk of loss or affectation of public assets or to establish the occurrence of events constituting liability and to collect and store evidence for the corresponding processes.

Table 2.1. Sectorial Delegate Comptrollers

Delegate Comptroller of the Agricultural Sector
Delegate Comptroller of the Mines and Energy Sector
Delegate Comptroller of the Health Sector
Delegate Comptroller of the Labour Sector
Delegate Comptroller of the Education, Science and Technology, Culture, Recreation and Sports Sector
Delegate Comptroller of the Social Inclusion Sector
Delegate Comptroller of the Infrastructure Sector
Delegate Comptroller of the Information and Communication Technologies Sector
Delegate Comptroller of the Housing and Basic Sanitation Sector
Delegate Comptroller of the Trade and Regional Development Sector
Delegate Comptroller of the Public Management and Financial Institutions Sector
Delegate Comptroller of the Defence and Security Sector
Delegate Comptroller of the Justice Sector
Delegate Comptroller of the Environment Sector

- The Departmental Management Offices are branches of the Comptroller's Office located in the country's departments in charge of controlling and surveillance of resources in the country's territories, under the direction of the Comptroller General. They were created in order for the CGR to have a presence throughout the national territory, strengthening fiscal control and efficiently carrying out prevention, investigation and punishment of acts of corruption and control of public management in the assigned territory. There are 31 Departmental Management Offices made up of a Departmental manager and no less than two provincial comptrollers (collegiate decision-making structure). Given that the preventive mechanism now includes 3 966 new control subjects at the territorial level, the Departmental Management Offices are central in the collection and monitoring of information related to preventive and concomitant control (DNP, 2021[1]). The implementation of this control over the new subjects is largely leveraged on the information compiled and provided by the Departmental Management Offices.

The fiscal surveillance directorates of the Sectorial Comptrollers' Offices and the fiscal surveillance groups of the Departmental Management Offices are in charge of the surveillance and control of fiscal management as developed by each of the control subjects forming part of the administration and of the individuals who handle state funds or assets. This work is carried out through different control actions, such as all types of audits and through special actions constituting of brief surveillance and control actions, in which an interdisciplinary working team addresses the investigation of a fact or matter brought to the attention of the CGR, by any means of information or by a citizen complaint (Contraloría General de la República de Colombia, 2021[2]).

Finally, through Decree 2037 of 2018, the Directorate of Information, Analysis and Immediate Reaction (DIARI) was created. The DIARI is a key element for preventive and concomitant control and, in general, in the digital transformation process of the CGR. The DIARI comprises the following units for Information, Information Analysis and Immediate Reaction:

- The *Information Unit* is in charge of managing the access, storage, security and administration of the information sources of the different public entities or individuals that administer public resources or carry out public functions. It also receives the source identification information required by the analysis unit and the Sectorial and General Delegate Comptrollers Offices. The information unit also conducts technical meetings with the entities to define and implement the technical mechanisms for connecting information sources and ensures improvements in data quality.

- The *Information Analysis Unit* designs and applies predictive and descriptive analytics models of the data provided by the information unit and carries out data analytics reports with alerts on risks of presumed detriment to public assets using, amongst others, "*big data*" techniques.
- The *Immediate Reaction Unit* acts according to the alerts raised by the Information Analysis Unit and carries out any special actions that may be required.

Promoting a strategy that integrates and leverages the work of the DIARI in relation to preventive and concomitant control

The use of artificial intelligence, analytics and data mining is becoming a fundamental tool for risk management and preventive control (OECD, 2019[3]). Making effective use of data and analysis requires more than simply introducing new tools, technologies or data sources into the work of audit institutions. It requires a strategy, with clear goals and objectives at all levels of the SAIs and in particular, a strategy that line managers and those in charge of implementation are aware of and can support. A data analytics strategy should be able to serve the public administration in guiding investments and other public decisions. A strategy also provides incentives for continuous learning and aligning data and analytics with long-term goals. Data and analytics serve institutional goals. Defining these goals and articulating them is a critical step in an organisation's digital transformation and instilling a culture that promotes decision-based analytics rather than data-driven decision making (Langhe and Puntoni, 2020[4]).

INTOSAI promotes the modernisation of SAIs by issuing standards and guidance that emphasise the critical role of data in supporting SAIs missions. Specifically, INTOSAI asks SAIs to take a strategic approach to how they use data. Several INTOSAI working groups and partners, such as the Information Technology Audit Working Group and the INTOSAI Development Initiative, have issued practical guidance on how SAIs can achieve this. The Guide to Combating Fraud and Corruption also highlights the critical role that data and analytics and suggests policies, practices and tools for leveraging data in support of this specific goal. There is no single definition of "analytics" (used as an abbreviation for "data analytics" in this report). Data analysis is a process of inspecting, cleaning, transforming and modelling data with the aim of discovering useful information, informing conclusions and supporting decision making (INTOSAI, 2019[5]).

The DIARI was created for this purpose. To this end, it comprises the aforementioned Information, Information Analysis and Immediate Reaction units to which functions related to preventive and concomitant control, among others, were assigned. In particular, Decree 403 of 2020 established that "fiscal surveillance and control activities must be supported by information management and the efficient use of all available technological capabilities."

Analytical models used by the DIARI to identify risks based on data

The DIARI uses a methodology for monitoring public resources based on information processing, the purpose of which is to produce data analytics reports and other reports and inputs on facts constituting alleged fiscal damage (Box 2.1). In the last year, the Analysis Unit deployed eight descriptive and predictive analytics initiatives to strengthen fiscal surveillance and control functions. Among them is a risk model for the processes in their contractual stage that involves descriptive data visualisation components allowing the characterisation of contracts, contractors and contracting parties. As such, dashboards were designed allowing the identification of the distribution patterns of the most prominent indicators, such as the frequency or value of contracts (Contraloría General de la República de Colombia, 2021[2]).

Box 2.1. Novell fiscal surveillance techniques in Colombia

The Directorate of Information, Analysis and Immediate Reaction (DIARI) of the Comptroller General of the Republic (CGR) of Colombia is made up of a multidisciplinary team of more than 130 people, trained in different disciplines. These people, according to their professional career and the entity's own needs, perform one or more roles with the following responsibilities:

- Connecting information sources, carrying out data quality processes, guaranteeing information security and managing connected sources.
- Quickly identifying the predictive value of information through exploratory analysis techniques, data processing and preparation.
- Managing structured or unstructured, geographic or alphanumeric data sets.
- Developing analytical models.

The DIARI makes intensive use of information technologies and related artificial intelligence to leverage the strategies and tactics of fiscal surveillance and control, whether preventive and concomitant, or *ex post*, supported by a robust physical infrastructure and logical architecture.

Among the products to be highlighted is the development of analytical models conceived as an abstract and reduced representation of phenomena resulting from the application of mathematical, statistical and computational techniques to associated data sets, in order to describe and explain their behaviour. Today, the DIARI has 22 analytical models.

For example, with the use of these technologies in the Public Works of Infrastructure Model, the CGR has managed to locate more than 2 000 infrastructure projects, including roads, educational institutions, hospitals, ports, airports and housing projects, among others, which are subject to surveillance and fiscal control.

Source: Information provided by CGR Colombia

Capitalising on the work of DIARI's Information Unit in strengthening data governance in Colombia

According to the interviews carried out for this report, both in the public sector and in civil society, one of the factors that most hinders the correct implementation of preventive and concomitant control is the disarticulation of public data. Indeed, there is currently no unified, homogenised and open information system in Colombia. This disarticulation implies that public entities and control bodies often have their own isolated information system and the availability and quality of data may vary significantly.

There are issues related to the construction and development of databases in the public administration. Human data-entry results in errors and inconsistencies (for example, in the use of names of entities or even numerical inconsistencies in the data itself). Added to this is the difficulty caused by the lack of harmonisation of databases and their interconnection (interoperability).

Thus, Decree 403 of 2020 generated tools for the CGR to advance data governance in Colombia. In particular, it establishes in Art. 57 (a) a mandate to the Information Unit of the DIARI to overcome barriers related to data quality.

To this end, this Unit leverages its data quality strategy in the "Data and Information Management and Governance System of the Office of the Comptroller General of the Republic", which aims to establish an appropriate orientation for the organisation, facilitating the efficient use of data and ultimately enabling business efficiency. To do this, it has organised its work into focuses, the main one being "data quality". To this end, it has assigned a "data quality manager" in charge of supporting the chief data officer (CDO) in establishing the data quality strategy, as well as supporting the dependencies and domain leaders in the execution of processes, design of controls, monitoring of plans, monitoring of compliance and activities aimed at improving data quality. This policy has been established in order to improve the use of data within public entities and to reduce the time and expenses associated with reconciling data.

In case of any need to remedy the quality of data produced internally, the Information Unit will determine the timescale for such remediation by the CDO depending on the impact on the CGR (reputational, operational and legal risks). In this way, domain leaders will be able to propose updates to the quality rules and quality thresholds for critical data elements based on business needs and historical information. These updates must be shared with the CGR's Data and Information Governance Committee.

The CGR reported that this process has been essential in the definition of a strategy for the implementation of technological tools that provide support, among others, related to the requirements of performing data cleaning, the production of data quality reports and feedback to the public administration regarding corresponding remedial actions. As such, the Information Unit holds workshops with the public administration, which allow them to communicate quality findings identified and thus have better response times for adjustments to information sources.

The CGR has made efforts to establish criteria for the presentation of information by financial managers, in compliance with Art. 57 (a) of the aforementioned Decree. In particular, through Circular 09 of 2020, a scheme was defined for working with all entities. The Circular includes information related to the form of access and disposition of the sources of information, as well as the possibility of holding workshops to define connection mechanisms, the information required by the CGR, the form of presentation and the transfer mechanism. In summary, the Information Unit currently has 5 420 sources of information from more than 683 entities.

One of the most noteworthy aspects of the DIARI and in particular of the Information Unit, is the role it plays in providing feedback to the public administration on the improvement of data. This feedback allows the entity to know which data are indeed relevant for preventive and concomitant control. In particular, data clean-up and feedback work, feedback sessions through workshops and data quality reports are a valuable by-product. In this sense, the CGR has set the goal of closing agreements for the consolidation of the 5 420 sources of information.

Consequently, the Information Unit has developed a unique vision on data management in Colombia, with significant contributions to data quality and management. This work has the potential to nurture data governance policy in Colombia on a larger scale.

To this end, the CGR could consider various actions as a producer and consumer of data:

- Measuring the progress of the quality of the data it receives and incorporating this component into the methodology of the Data Governance Model currently being designed.
- Promoting, via workshops with the public administration and based on the technologies used by DIARI, the standardisation of a database model that allows the interoperability of high volumes of information, in such a way as to facilitate its automation.
- Promoting, through the current spaces of interaction (workshops and feedback reports), the automation of all processes by the entities, in order to have structured and better quality data.
- Working on the cleaning of data and feedback with other actors - including at the territorial level - private administrators and parafiscal funds. To this end, it could demand high quality standards in data reported via government mechanisms.

- Communicating internally and externally the role of the "Data and Information Governance Committee" in such a way that it helps in the unification of the technological standard throughout the Comptrollers' Offices, facilitating the interaction of internal data.

- Based on the model of the CGR's Data Governance Committee, ensuring that the public administration defines the design and implementation of an intersectorial committee (governing body) for the management and quality of data for all entities, in such a way that it helps in the unification of the technological standard throughout the entire Colombian public administration.

Strengthening the role of the Analysis Unit in risk analysis and giving it improved tools for its management

The data compiled by the Information Unit is communicated to the Analysis Unit for the construction of analytical models. These reports generally contain alerts about suspected fiscal damages. The Analysis Unit produces this information in relation to its own criteria and upon any necessary request by the General, Sectorial and Territorial Delegate Comptrollers. The Analysis Unit also provides support to these offices on the use of the model.

This is done based on advanced analytics models, which address the most recurrent business questions or general management issues with the greatest impact. To do this, it designs and executes the most appropriate analytical strategies to address working hypotheses, defines descriptive or predictive objectives, traces the data preparation route, information modelling and architecture and other analytical functions. Finally, it evaluates the results of the data mining process and contrasts them with the proposed objectives, carrying out a statistical and quality-based validation in accordance with the requirements of the end users of each of the models (Contraloría General de la República de Colombia, 2021[2]).

To this end, the Analysis Unit has various roles within the CGR. On the one hand, it provides support to the Sectorial, General and Territorial Delegate Comptrollers in the crossing of data for the support of audits. On the other hand, it produces reports where imminent risk of loss of public resources and/or negative impact on patrimonial assets is detected, which are delivered to the Sectorial, General and Territorial Delegate Comptrollers and the DIARI Immediate Reaction Unit. Finally, it produces dashboards, which help resolve recurring questions or work hypotheses prioritised by the CGR mission teams and provides support and technical assistance to the end users of the models.

Specialised teams in data analytics within SAI to reinforce risk identification

Specialised groups for data analytics, such as DIARI's Analysis Unit, have created new opportunities to assess the risks of fraud and corruption in various countries. For example, the Korea Fair Trade Commission uses the Bidding Manipulation Indicator Analysis System (BRIAS) to analyse large volumes of data from Korean public entities and create a probability score for bid rigging. In Chile, the government uses data mining from the electronic procurement system to prevent collusion and favouritism. In the United Kingdom, Italy and Turkey there are also examples of the use of analytics groups for risk identification, as well as the design of methodologies for the use of analytics in the development of audits (Box 2.2). Such efforts have developed rapidly in recent decades, as governments embrace digital strategies and take advantage of open data, "big data" tools and data analytics (OECD, 2019[3]).

Box 2.2. Examples of using analytics in SAIs

United Kingdom

The United Kingdom's National Audit Office (NAO) established a Data Service to meet the demands of auditors that routinely need access to large volumes of data. This team maintains a number of large datasets, stores them in NAO's data warehouse and merges them for auditors to use and interpret. The Data Service also provides guidance for audit teams that are using the data, which can be accessed through a common Share Point site. The Methods, Economics and Statistics Hub (MESH) complements the Data Service. This community of practice leads the NAO's work on analytics and big data, and it co-ordinates across a range of specialist areas to provide training and financial support for audits and wider assurance work. In addition to data analysis and analytics, MESH's areas of expertise include economics, statistics, modelling, mapping, and qualitative analysis.

Italy

The Italian Court of Audit (*Corte dei Conti*, CdC) developed a "Data Analysis Competency Centre," which became a cross-functional team and brings together business and technical competencies to support the effective implementation of SIDIF-ConosCo. The Centre supports users of SIDIF-ConosCo to make better decisions using machine learning, analytics, predictive analysis and other data analytics techniques. This Centre is in the early stages of its development and intends to be a multi-disciplinary team with knowledge and skills that span levels of government (i.e. national and regional) as well as technologies. According to CdC officials, this effort signals a recognition that any data-driven tool is not static, and requires a capacity-building strategy to support its development and evolution.

Turkey

In 2017, the Turkish Court of Accounts (TCA) created a "Data Analysis Group" to design methodologies for using computer-assisted audit techniques (CAAT) and enhance the capability of the TCA to assess risks in municipalities. The group had other aims, including decreasing auditors' workload, analysing big data, identifying mistakes and errors in data processing, and automation of analyses to facilitate continuous monitoring. Their efforts resulted in "VERA", TCA's Data Analysis and Business Intelligence System, which automates risk analysis for over 1 400 municipalities to inform audit programming and planning.

Source: (U.K. National Audit Office, 2019[6]), (House of Commons, United Kingdom, 2017[7]), (Court of Auditors, 2019[8]), OECD Interviews with public officials from the CdC.

Strengthening the external and internal relationship of the DIARI through the use of tools produced by the Analysis Unit

The reliability and accuracy of risk assessments is a fundamental challenge for both the audit body and the auditees. In theory, data analytics should be able to enable financial managers to identify risky transactions as well as adapt control activities throughout the cycle of the project, including predicting high-risk transactions before committing funds (OECD, 2019[3]).

To this end, and as observed in the interviews carried out for this report, the Analysis Unit could still have great potential to leverage co-operation processes both internally and externally, but this merits reinforcement. Firstly, during the interviews, it was observed that the main focus of the Analysis Unit was identifying shortcomings related to the monitoring of the budget chain (cost overruns, execution time and other procedural aspects). However, the identification of risks in public administration, the feedback of early warnings information to entities, as well as the predictive analytics exercises are still in a primary stage. Secondly, communication with the General, Sectorial and Territorial Delegate Comptrollers deserves special attention, to the extent that there is reprocessing in requests for information to public entities, alongside scant feedback between the parties. Finally, even though the DIARI has carried out information cross-checks and obtained the meshes requested by the Departmental Management Offices, the interviews conducted for this report found evidence of lack of communication with the territorial level, where products received were said to be basic or difficult to understand (such as highly complex contracting meshes without any prior analysis). It is in this sense that the Analysis Unit should work on strengthening and better communicate the delivery of products in accordance with territorial needs.

As such, strengthening the data analytics strategy should be considered to yield the results required by the audit teams. To do this, an internal and external client identification exercise could be used. This inventory could contain internal and external allies that promote a balanced increase of capacities for the use of data and analytics. As such, the CGR could adopt a unified, cohesive and strategic approach on data analytics to maximise resources, improve decision making and achieve the objectives of the organisation, as seen in Brazil or Australia (Box 2.3).

Box 2.3. Development of policy and systems for the use of analytics in SAIs

Brazil: Information-Based Governance and Solutions

Brazil's supreme audit institution (*Tribunal de Contas da União*, TCU) developed its own analytical capacity with a strategic decision to decentralise its analytical capacities to the audit teams. Departments trained auditors in data analytics, encouraged them to seek data and technology support tools that would be useful for their audits and formed communities of practice.

Analytics can facilitate decision making related to the selection of audits, but the increasing amount of information and the seemingly endless possibilities for analysis can often hamper efforts toward efficiency and effectiveness. Therefore, institutions must formalise and implement work processes to ensure that the analyses actually improve the body's work, that the information used is necessary and sufficient to fulfil its purpose.

Brazil's supreme audit institution did this by focusing on three pillars:

- Governance: the guidance, support and direction from top management, including a cohesive organisational strategy and action plan. This can help create a culture within the organisation that encourages the use of analytics for control activities.
- Platform: the tangible tools necessary to execute analytics-related tasks, to obtain useful information from raw data. For example, TCU established and manages a virtual environment called "*Labcontas*" that allows auditors to access easily and independently information from dozens of databases as a benefit of agreements signed between public institutions. This facilitates co-ordination of efforts and reduces the time and resources often required to obtain information during audits.
- Information-based solutions: The tools and high-level structures in place must result in actionable, timely and reliable insights. This type of information is used in Brazil for a variety of audit-related tasks, from holding managers accountable to flagging potential high-risk grants or procurement proposals submitted to the government.

Australia: a unified approach to data analytics

Australia has adopted a unified, cohesive and strategic approach to data analytics for audit institutions hoping to maximise resources, improve decision making and achieve organisational goals. With this in mind, the Australian National Audit Office (ANAO) annual corporate plan sets out a clear and concise framework on how technology and data analytics will be used in the organisation, the specific and relevant processes in place and which teams across the organisation are responsible for each aspect.

More specifically, the document identifies a stand-alone team dedicated to analytics, key areas in which the Office would like to use data to better meet its objectives, and ways in which it would like to improve data governance practices. The importance of data analytics to the organisation's work is also highlighted by its mention in other related sections of the corporate plan, including those on human capital, budgeting and productivity.

Source: (Revista do TCU, 2016[9]); (Australian National Audit Office, 2020[10])

Similarly, in Turkey for example, the VERA system provides auditees with a standard and automated tool for the risk-based classification of more than 1 400 municipalities (Box 2.4).

Box 2.4. Data analytics and organisational intelligence system in Turkey

The Turkish Court of Accounts (TCA) created "VERA", a Data Analysis and Business Intelligence System, which automates risk analysis for over 1 400 municipalities to inform audit programming and planning. VERA provides auditees a standard, automated tool for risk-based ranking of over 1 400 municipalities. VERA allows management to take into account risks before the TCA's annual audit programming and supports the creation of the audit strategy.

In addition, auditors use the results of the risk analyses to plan audits, as well as identify possible material misstatements in financial reports that could represent errors and fraud. All auditors have access to VERA, and are able to assess the results of VERA's automated analyses related to risks and financial indicators in a dashboard or automatically generated reports.

Source: (OECD, forthcoming[11])

Making use of new techniques for data analytics that contribute to strengthening preventive and concomitant control

Developing an action plan to monitor new and existing analytical initiatives is critical to the success of SAI. The CGR is primarily a consumer of data and the models and systems it develops to run analytics are subject to change over time. This may include changes in the quality or relevance of the data depending on the methodology. Changes in context, data reliability or data access can affect the accuracy and usefulness of any model. For this reason, continuous monitoring of the performance of data and analytics initiatives should be a critical component.

The use of new data analytics techniques, in which the DIARI is specialised, is essential for the success of preventive and concomitant control. For example, in relation to "big data" techniques, these can be a valuable addition to the analysis of audit information, particularly when rigorous analytical procedures are combined with appropriate audit techniques and experts (Gepp et al., 2018[12]). The value of integrating "big data" into audit analysis enables the development of new skills. In particular, in instructing analysts on which data to obtain from the information and its use by mission areas (General, Sectorial and Territorial Delegate Comptrollers Offices), as well as the ability to permeate the entire audit process, allowing auditors to get used to its functionalities (Gepp et al., 2018[12]; EY, 2015[13]). Figure 2.2 shows the experience of the UK National Audit Office (NAO) in relation to its data analytics strategy. In particular, it focuses on data mining processes and on reducing costs to administrations by detecting patterns and anomalies.

For this reason, the CGR could consider adopting tools aimed at preventive work in the future, through predictive analytical models to identify risks. This work, in turn, can be leveraged on the use of prospective models based on data analytics and incorporate the available information within the different areas of the CGR, as well as that produced, for example, by performance audits and sector studies. For this, it could also use international experiences as references, such as those of the United Kingdom shown in Figure 2.2 and could establish and maintain a quantitative risk assessment framework that is efficient and can be used effectively in risk management.

Figure 2.2. Data analytics at the UK National Audit Office (NAO)

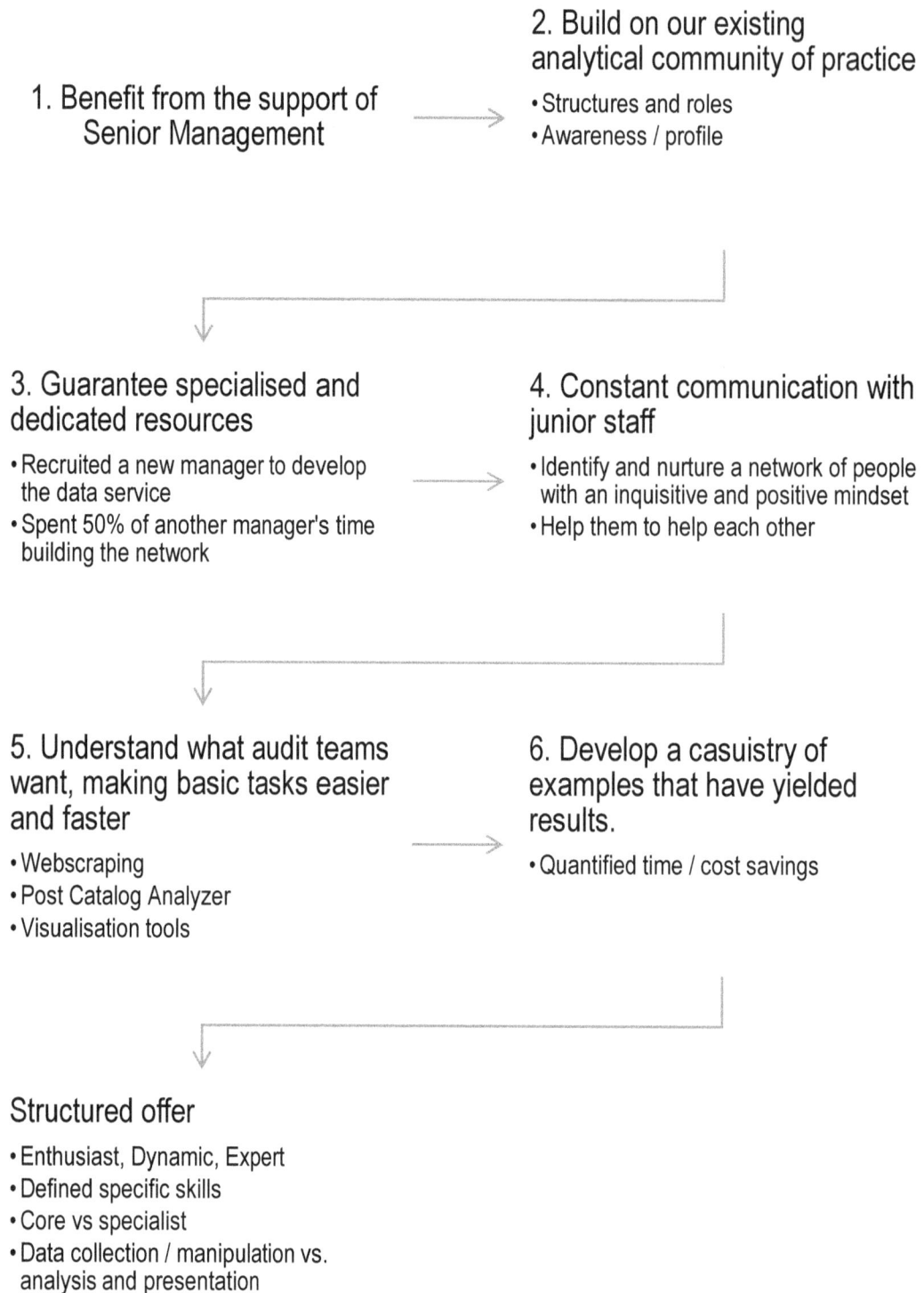

1. Benefit from the support of Senior Management

2. Build on our existing analytical community of practice
- Structures and roles
- Awareness / profile

3. Guarantee specialised and dedicated resources
- Recruited a new manager to develop the data service
- Spent 50% of another manager's time building the network

4. Constant communication with junior staff
- Identify and nurture a network of people with an inquisitive and positive mindset
- Help them to help each other

5. Understand what audit teams want, making basic tasks easier and faster
- Webscraping
- Post Catalog Analyzer
- Visualisation tools

6. Develop a casuistry of examples that have yielded results.
- Quantified time / cost savings

Structured offer
- Enthusiast, Dynamic, Expert
- Defined specific skills
- Core vs specialist
- Data collection / manipulation vs. analysis and presentation

Source: Data Analytics at the NAO (intosaipas.org)

In summary, the potential of the Analysis Unit could be explored through the following considerations:

- Develop a unified vision for data and analytics, including one that reflects audit and governance trends related to big data. This policy vision can be included and aligned with the next National Development Plan (*PND, Plan Nacional de Desarrollo*), providing broader objectives for digital transformation, including delineating a theory of change to contribute to good governance and accountability in the public sector, as well as positioning the CGR as a national and international example of high quality technical expertise (Chapter 4).

- Establish indicators and a theory of change with respect to data and analysis, focusing on results and not simply outputs (for example, indicators that reflect the prevention, mitigation or recovery of losses as a result of data and analysis).

- Develop an action plan to ensure the relevance of its analytical initiatives and the reliability of results, particularly for the new methodologies and systems that are under development. This action plan may focus on corporate objectives to leverage data and analysis to improve audit work. Using the data governance framework outlined above to help frame key areas to focus on and identify priorities, where it is important to consider the implications and relevance of data analytics to the entire audit cycle, as well as considering the internal context and the fact that activities are tailored to the purpose of individual teams within the CGR.

- Adopt tools aimed at preventive work, including the identification of risks in public administration, as well as the adequate communication of them to public managers. This work can in turn leverage the use of prospective models and incorporate information available within the different areas of the CGR (such as that produced, for example, by performance audits and sector studies).

- Promote learning, inclusion and experimentation when using data and new techniques, including the development of a baseline to measure the impact of the CGR in relation to the new data analytics strategies and in relation to its results and advantages.

- Raise awareness among CGR officials about data analytics and how it contributes to risk analysis in order to develop technical capacities and promote the specialisation of personnel.

- Generate internal co-ordination through meetings between the DIARI and the General, Sectorial and Territorial Delegate Comptrollers' Offices in order to identify and make use of the internal information of the CGR, including audit reports from previous years (Box 2.5), in such a way that these audits are integrated as data input into the system.

- Articulate with the territorial level so that they have access so the same information shared with other dependencies of the CGR, in particular through the establishment of links and the strengthening of capacities in the Departmental Management Offices.

Box 2.5. Learning from history: Using previous reports and sectorial studies as sources of information

Some Supreme Audit Institutions (SAI) use the evidence in their reports as input to develop good practice guides.

- The UK National Audit Office (NAO) published its good practice guide for commercial contract management in 2021 based on findings and recommendations from 209 reports published over the last 20 years. The guide incorporates recent audits of commercial contracts related to COVID-19.

- The Comptroller General of the Republic of Peru identified the main causes of delays in ten public works projects, executed with the Public-Private Partnerships (PPP) model. The study concludes with recommendations to prevent delays in future projects, which could serve as criteria applicable to future PPPs. The methodology was based on a PPP literature review, on interviews with PPP officials and specialists, on the selection of a sample of PPP contracts, using criteria of accessibility, heterogeneity, amount and an analysis of contracts additions to identify causes of renegotiation. The findings show that close to 50% of the additions were signed before three years, compared to the average term of the concessions of 27 years. In addition, about 20% of the additions were the product of non-compliance by the State (the grantor) with the deadlines for land reclamation and lack of access to water. Also, at the time of the contract design, the basic engineering, environmental and geological studies were often not available, which affected the allocation of risks. Thus, the study recommends avoiding delays in the delivery of land by the State, ensuring that before the beginning of the process, the land is properly cleaned up and that there are updated and reliable studies to avoid cost increases.

Source: https://www.nao.org.uk/report/good-practice-guidance-for-managing-the-commercial-lifecycle/; (CGR Perú, 2015[14])

Optimising the functions of DIARI's Immediate Reaction Unit (URI) in such a way that it contributes more than special control actions to strengthen inter-institutional relations for preventive and concomitant control

The Immediate Reaction Unit (URI) is in charge of closing the cycle of review, analysis and data use. In particular, it can issue alerts based on the reports of the Analysis Unit, as well as advise and guide immediate reaction activities. As such, the URI executes on-site verifications of unfinished public works through the use of monitoring technologies (drones, satellites, among others).

For the purposes of preventive and concomitant control, the URI is in charge of the "special control action", which is a brief fiscal control action, constituting a rapid response to a fact or matter that may come to the attention of the CGR through the SACI, once the system will be in operation. This action can also be started through citizen's complaints or by identifying concerning issues through social media.

Therefore, the URI has received 302 alerts on contracts with alleged cost overruns, within the framework of the health emergency caused by COVID-19 and issued by the Information Analysis Unit (Contraloría General de la República de Colombia, 2021[2]). These alerts were distributed to internal dependencies of the CGR and to other control entities for their knowledge and processing. As such, the URI has strong links with the public administration and, in particular, provides a fundamental feedback service to the public administration through these alerts. It does this through risk reports, as well as workshops with the public administration and citizens.

However, the URI has not yet reached the level of maturity needed to generate more preventive alerts. According to the CGR, this is because there are still no criteria to determine whether the cases made available to them and brought to its knowledge are considered sensitive or if they have some other classification. That is, the alerts that are raised with the URI are made under criteria of importance or relevance for the region, project value and the similar alerted situations, but not based on a risk analysis.

Supporting transformation processes which allow the internal appropriation of preventive and concomitant control

Preventive and concomitant control, as a new and developing tool, still has opportunities for improvement and appropriation among CGR officials. An example of this was given during the interviews conducted for this report where several actors referred to the "alerts" as part of the *ex post* control or where several officials expressed their concern about the lack of training on this new tool. The need for clarification and a truly differentiated approach became evident in the call by various officials to set up special groups for the preventive control or to include the preventive perspective into the Sectorial Delegate Comptrollers. In particular, several of the interviewees mentioned that a large part of the CGR officials involved in preventive and concomitant control have a vision focused on the culture of "findings" *(hallazgos)*, where "*alerts*" or "*warnings*" are perceived as a process focused on detecting cases and requiring investigative work to eventually implement a fiscal responsibility process.

In addition, there was evidence of a tendency to analyse complaints and information on issues related exclusively to acts of corruption, including the so-called "white elephants" or processes where cost overruns are evident in public procurement. Even though these actions are essential for the CGR's work in the fight against corruption, as already emphasised, preventive control has the potential to generate more structural positive changes within the public administration. In this sense, its usefulness should be strengthened in matters such as risk management and improvement of processes and procedures associated with fiscal management.

Resolution 762 of 2020, Art. 38 had already highlighted the need to establish working groups for concomitant and preventive control. In particular, it assigned to the General and Sectorial Delegate Comptrollers a Concomitant and Preventive Control Working Group attached to the office of the respective Delegate and made up of a minimum of three public servants with an exclusive mandate for the development of the functions of the group. As such, the general functions of the Concomitant and Preventive Control Working Group would be supported by the Directorates of Fiscal Surveillance or Sectorial Studies or the Directorate of Regional Surveillance, Promotion and Development of Citizen Control. Currently, there are some officials who are in charge of monitoring the "alerts" as well as fiscal surveillance and permanent monitoring to identify situations that should be communicated to other CGR dependencies, other control entities or to the public. Additionally, the constitution of these working groups has not prevented the existing organisational structure from advancing or being able to carry out preventive and concomitant control exercises.

To this end, and taking into consideration the provisions of Legislative Act 4 of 2019, Law Decree 403 of 2020, Resolution 762 of 2020 and the internal procedure adopted, the CGR should strive to develop actions aimed at:

- Overcoming silos to strengthen preventive oversight and improve communication and internal exchange.
- Taking advantage of the new preventive and concomitant control to strengthen sectorial studies and performance audits.
- Promoting behavioural and cultural change, leveraged on the current institutional framework of the CGR, which helps to understand and internalise the preventive function among the CGR, the public administration and the citizens.

Strengthening internal exchange and communication to break "silos" and ensure the effectiveness and efficiency of preventive and concomitant control

During the interviews, there was clarity about the need to increase internal communication between the different areas of the CGR related to preventive and concomitant control to ensure that the new function is properly understood and appropriated and misunderstandings with other mechanisms avoided. These challenges in internal co-ordination are undoubtedly based on a cultural change and the appropriation of the mechanism, but also from an appropriate understanding of the conceptual and practical differences between "alerts", which in most cases are generated correctively and "warnings" that seek, as stated by the Law and the Constitutional Court, to have more of a preventive approach (Chapter 1). In addition, the analysis of the information provided by the CGR and the interviews carried out, evidenced the fragmentation of criteria and the existence of silos in relation to preventive and concomitant control within the CGR.

The silo mentality is a recurring problem in the implementation of new processes across all organisations and is characterised by individuals or divisions that hide information from others in the organisation for one or more reasons. These may include power struggles, fear, organisational inefficiency, or simply may be due to the fact that no effort is made to update shared information. Also, historical labour relations ("it has always been like this here") and organisational micro cultures ("this unit doesn't work like us") can contribute to exacerbate the problem. The silo mind-set destroys trust, cuts off communications and encourages complacency. An isolated organisation cannot act quickly or seize opportunities. When information is not freely shared, informed and evidence-based decisions cannot be made (Froy and Giguère, 2010[15]). Breaking these resistances saves time and allows the entity's objectives to be achieved.

These silos refer to the refinement of internal processes and procedures. In particular, the interaction between the DIARI and the Sectorial Delegate Comptrollers (and with the Delegate of Citizen Participation) should be strengthened and designed with more clarity. In addition, the interviews conducted indicated the need for greater integration with the Departmental Management Offices, who have the need to access not only the information produced by the DIARI, but also to improve their interaction with the Sectorial Delegate Comptrollers.

A positive aspect observed during the interviews refers to the informal arrangements between the General and Sectorial Delegate Comptrollers that currently guide the process. Several of the interviewees established that this informal co-ordination has allowed them to refine criteria and learn from previous decisions made by other Delegates in similar processes.

However, this informal co-ordination could benefit from some additional formal arrangements. In particular, such an institutionalisation would be key for the generation of institutional memory within the entity and for the unification of performance criteria.

In this regard, the CGR could consider incorporating the following recommendations:

- **Creating a unified vision of preventive and concomitant control** that overcomes divisions within the CGR, both at the national and territorial levels, establishing goals that benefit multiple agencies and territorial levels. Among others, ensure that each General, Sectorial and Territorial Delegate is not only focused on achieving their specific objectives with isolated information, but on the contrary, this information must be shared between teams. For this, it is essential to strengthen the relationship between decision makers and area leaders, as well as to encourage work groups with officials from various agencies.
- **Educate, work and train.** One way to break down silos is to educate, work and train together on exercises that include different dependencies. Collaborative training across divisions is a way to combine required training with collaborative silo-breaking practices.
- **Frequent internal communication.** Another way to break silos is to generate constant communication spaces, formally and informally, where information is made available, as well as the generation of feedback exercises between different units of the CGR. For example, this could be achieved by encouraging communication exercises with Departmental Management Offices and providing case studies that differentiate the preventive function from *ex post* control.

To ensure good co-ordination between the different dependencies of the CGR, the following could be analysed:

- Include in the procedure for the implementation of concomitant and preventive control (Process VIG 01 PR 001) casuistic guides from previous activity and relevant international practices.
- Improve understanding of the new control by conducting seminars or workshops on specific cases that serve to illustrate concomitant and preventive control. In these seminars or workshops, the Sectorial Delegate Comptrollers will be able to share information and experiences.
- Analyse the potential for an internal, non-binding committee, where some of the most relevant cases, risks identified and best ways to understand the different situations are discussed. In particular, this committee could count on input not only from the areas directly involved, but also from other relevant actors where applicable.
- Continue with the feedback exercises of the General, Sectorial and Territorial Delegate Comptrollers to the DIARI in relation to the usefulness, relevance and usage of the information the DIARI produces. For example, it could be very useful for the DIARI to receive feedback on whether this information is useful for scheduling audits, whether it should be more focused on x or y aspect or on whether the reports should more clearly indicate risks). As such, the DIARI could have closer communication with different areas of the CGR, including the Departmental Management Offices, by sharing the analysis reports they produce, as well as providing training on how to use them and on how to interpret the information produced.
- Analyse the possibility of creating a specialised unit to allow the intersectoral analysis of the information collected by the Sectorial Delegate Comptrollers for the purposes of preventive and concomitant control. This will make it possible to homogenise the type of information received by the Comptroller General for the purposes of the warning mechanism and to differentiate the interaction of the Sectorial Delegate Comptrollers with the public administration for purposes other than fiscal control. Ultimately, this will make it possible to differentiate the sanction-related from the preventive work in the relationships with public entities.
- Consider establishing concomitant and preventive control working groups, as provided in Resolution 762 of 2020, Art. 38 and in accordance with the needs of the CGR and the Sectorial Comptrollers' Offices.

Taking advantage of the new preventive and concomitant control to strengthen sectorial studies and performance audits

Performance audits seek to provide information, analysis and recommendations for improvements in public policy planning (INTOSAI, 2019[16]). In particular, they aim to improve the management of the public sector and report on how many of its recommendations are accepted and applied by the public administration. Thus, performance audits follow a different logic than the more traditional role of fiscal control bodies, since they evaluate the policy design from its conception, identifying design flaws and whether it is at odds with macro policy objectives. In this way, performance audits are clearly framed within the concept of preventive control as they seek the same objectives. Furthermore, the information produced by these performance audits may eventually also inform preventive and concomitant control work.

The CGR has a mandate to carry out performance audits through Article 119 and 267 of the Political Constitution, which establishes that "the Office of the Comptroller General of the Republic is in charge of the surveillance and control of fiscal management of the administration". As such, Art. 124 of Law 1474 of 2011 states that "the regulation of the methodology of the auditing process by the CGR and the other comptrollers will take into account the instrumental condition of regular audits with respect to performance audits, with a view to guaranteeing a comprehensive exercise of the auditing function". In addition, Decree 1499 of 2017 establishes the guidelines of the Quality Management System as a systematic and transparent management tool to allow the management and evaluation of institutional performance in terms of quality and social satisfaction in the provision of services. In interviews conducted for this report, it became clear that there is still scope for improvement. This is, because the system cannot really determine if institutional policies being analysed in the framework of performance audits, operate in accordance with the principles of economy, efficiency and effectiveness or if there are areas of improvement of these public policies within public institutions.

This situation is exacerbated due to several circumstances within the CGR. Performance audits are located in the micro areas of the Sectorial Delegate Comptrollers that is, in the area of fiscal surveillance. Several experts have already mentioned that a weakness of the current system is that the fiscal surveillance departments follow the logic of "sanction" and "compliance" rather than being result oriented (Inter-American Development Bank, 2019[17]). Multiple experts interviewed for this report have also identified several shortcomings in the current institutional arrangement. Among others, the areas in charge do not have the horizontal vision for the implementation of public policies and this, in turn, is reflected in the profile of the officials in charge. This distorts the preventive work and feedback to the entity. This vision was confirmed by the evaluation of the Performance Measurement Framework (*Marco Medición del Desempeño, MMD*) that was carried out in the CGR between 2017 and 2018, as well as during the update of guidelines to implement part of the recommendations for closing performance gaps (Inter-American Development Bank, 2019[17]).

In particular, these documents recommended giving the Sectorial Studies Directorates (*Direccciones de Estudios Sectoriales*, DES) authority over performance audits. This, under the understanding that the DES have the experience and specific capacity to carry out evaluations of public policies. The Constitutional reform brought by Legislative Act 04 of 2019 included the modification of some of the mechanisms to deepen the analysis of public policies and sectorial behaviour of the DES, bringing a unique opportunity to transfer this function to these areas, as they have the necessary skills to carry out performance audits. In addition, this mechanism could be strengthened through the information produced by the DIARI.

Furthermore, performance audits can support citizen participation strategies that in turn generate institutional benefits and strengthen public trust. Social organisations can be valuable allies of the CGR, using their experience and networks throughout the performance audit process and becoming valuable stakeholders. This is especially the case for policies aiming, for example, to achieving the sustainable development objectives (SDG), since the audits will ultimately reflect a citizen vision for control and therefore contribute to the sustainability of the public policies being audited.

The CGR has taken important steps to improve the institutional framework related to performance audits. In compliance with the CGR improvement plan, the CGR advanced the final verification of the update of the Performance Audit Guide, focused on auditing government programmes, projects, systems, operations, activities or organisations, to deem whether they operate in accordance with the principles of economy, efficiency and effectiveness. In addition to these changes, in the new version of the Performance Audits Guide, the criteria and standards of ISSAI 300 (3000, 3910 and 3920) and Decree Law 403 of 2020 have been incorporated. Once approved, the guide may impact the growth of performance audits considerably in the 2022 period.

To this end, the CGR could consider the following actions to strengthen performance audits, to complement and leverage preventive and concomitant control:

- Give the mandate for performance audits to the DES, as part of the evaluation process of public policies, which today are in charge of the DES, ensuring co-ordination with the fiscal surveillance areas as appropriate, given that DES are more familiar with the development of analysis and research in sectorial studies.
- Advance the updating of the new Performance Audit Guide, where the criteria and standards of ISSAIS 300 (3000, 3910 and 3920) and Decree Law 403 of 2020 are incorporated.
- Adjust the profiles required by the DES and in particular, the personal in charge of performance audits as well as provide the available positions on the areas of performance audits.
- Consolidate a team of mentors to carry out training programmes in performance audits, ensuring that those who receive the training have the appropriate profile.
- Develop a strategy for citizen participation that in turn contributes to the SDG through mechanisms of dialogue, participation and accountability with citizens, which reflect a citizen vision for control and provide sustainability to audited public policies.

As such, as recommended in Chapter 1, one substantial advance would be for the CGR to be able to issue recommendations to the public administration to contribute to improve performance-related results. Such recommendations should not to be equated with co-administration. Currently, as mentioned before, the CGR does not issue recommendations of any kind due to the perception that this would be co-administration. However, the CGR could consider regulating this mechanism. As mentioned, many SAIs around the world use the evidence found in performance audits to formulate recommendations. Box 2.6 shows the experience of the United States Government Accountability Office (GAO) in this area.

Box 2.6. Effective use of recommendations in performance audits

The United States Government Accountability Office (GAO) was able to significantly reduce fraud in the COVID-19 relief programme by providing recommendations to the entities managing the emergency. The report, prepared in less than 90 days, presents relevant, sufficient and reliable evidence that supports the recommendations, including the recovery of incorrect payments to deceased persons and new legislation to prevent fraud.

The report to Congress describes (1) the government's activities to support individuals; (2) estimates of the aid distributed; (3) the responsible ministries; and (4) the effectiveness of internal control in the ministries to prevent and detect errors and fraud in payments. The methodology included: interviews with ministries; analysis of previous audits by the GAO and internal control offices in the responsible ministries; analysis of expenses and people who received the aid and a review of the corresponding documents.

Among the recommendations issued are the following:

1. That the Internal Revenue Service (IRS), the US tax agency, send notifications to the beneficiaries, requesting that they return payments designated for deceased persons.
2. That Congress amend the law so that the IRS can obtain early and expeditious access to the Social Security Administration (SSA) file of persons deceased.

To this end, there was a follow-up to recommendations, taking into account that the IRS reported that it recovered 57% of the payments sent to deceased persons and that, in effect, Congress approved the legislation that requires the Ministry of the Treasury to access the file of persons deceased for a period of three years.

Source: GAO-20-625, Accessible Version, COVID-19: Opportunities to Improve Federal Response and Recovery Efforts

---

Promote cultural change within the CGR and the public administration for a collaborative, preventive and transparent vision of fiscal management

Part of the success of the new preventive and concomitant control will depend on the appropriation of the mechanism, which requires an understanding of the substantial differences between a supervisory task and a preventive task, as well as the generation of internal capacities that point to preventive work, not only to a more timely detection of problems or to sanctioning. As within all organisations, it is the officials who are the final decision makers, who implement the regulatory framework and therefore are the ones who determine its success. Cultural change then becomes one of the most important engines of change for the success of the new preventive and concomitant mechanism.

The CGR has made a significant effort to respond to this challenge. During 2020 and 2021, socialisation activities have been carried out through seminars, guaranteeing that 90% of the entity will be trained in various relevant subjects. However, the CGR's senior management recognises that it is important to continue the efforts to raise the awareness of officials on all the operational details related to preventive and concomitant control. To this end, a dedicated strategy has been designed within the CGR aimed at strengthening the preventive and concomitant control so that CGR officials know, master, understand and apply the tools provided by the Constitution, the law and the regulations on the new model of fiscal control in Colombia.

However, despite these efforts, in the interviews conducted for this report, several of the interviewees spoke not only of the need to generate capacities, through training and capacity building for the preventive perspective, but also of the need to promote larger-scale cultural change in the CGR. The informal standard that a good audit is one which produces many "findings and observations" still seems to dominate within the CGR and influences the behaviour of auditors.

As such, it is important for the CGR to continue its training efforts with an effective awareness-raising and capacity-building programme around risk management in general, with a specific module on fraud and corruption risk management, taking advantage of the variety of already existing programmes. For example, training should be delivered as part of induction or orientation programmes. In addition, the CGR could consider:

- Continuing training and education for the Sectorial, General and Territorial Delegate Comptrollers on the scope of preventive and concomitant control, as well as on the use of the information produced by the DIARI. The training could even be extended to include risk analysis and management of public administration, examining the capacity of the latter to achieve expected results.
- Making use of the Centre for Fiscal Studies (*Centro de Estudios Fiscales*, CEF), which is in charge of high-quality training in matters of surveillance and control in the management of public resources, to carry out internal training processes on the tasks of preventive control, including the identification and management of fraud and corruption risks.

However, training is not enough to generate changes in the behaviour and culture of organisations (OECD, 2018[18]). In fact, auditors are part of social groups, which may be their audit unit or the SAI in which they work, or even the auditing profession as a whole. What auditors believe most auditors in their reference group are doing (empirical expectation) or what they believe most auditors in their group expect them to do (normative expectation) may explain their patterns of behaviour. These beliefs are called "social norms" and can be extremely powerful in shaping behaviours (Bicchieri, 2017[19]; Bicchieri, 2005[20]).

This is why changing social norms so that they impact organisational cultures is complex, takes time and is a gradual process, but it is also key to generating sustainable changes (Yamin et al., 2019[21]). The strategies that can be used to generate changes in the organisational culture associated with preventive and concomitant control are various and the CGR could consider applying the BASIC methodology (*Behaviour, Analysis, Strategy, Intervention, Change*), developed by the OECD to apply a behavioural perspective to public policy. Thus, the CGR could identify and analyse behaviours of its public officials that prevent the appropriation of new preventive control and develop strategies to induce change (OECD, 2019[22]).

The application of behavioural insights to organisations demonstrates the importance of influencing specific individuals to achieve changes throughout the organisation and to intervene directly in the organisational routines, policies and procedures (OECD, 2020[23]). Box 2.7 provides an overview of some key theoretical foundations and insights from organisational psychology when it comes to influencing organisational behaviour.

Box 2.7. Applying Behavioural Insights to Organisations: Theoretical Foundations

When enough people are nudged toward behavioural change, those new behaviours have the potential to become habit, switching from deliberate choices and actions otherwise known as controlled processing, to less deliberate, less effortful, more habitual actions known as automatic processing. Whether deliberate or effortful, choice or habit, when enough people in a work group or entire organisation behave in a certain way, that behaviour has the potential to become a norm. Norms are rules for expected and accepted behaviour. As humans, violating norms tends to make us uncomfortable. We are likely to conform to the norms of our work group and organisation. This is especially true of cohesive groups who feel a degree of attraction to their work group.

Nudging supervisors or other powerful or influential people within an organisation can have a multiplying effect such that the behaviours exhibited and endorsed by influential individuals have a better chance of being adopted *en masse*, nudging a whole organisation in the process. Indeed, charismatic and transformational leaders are believed to possess qualities that inspire followers to behave in desired ways in service of a larger goal. Nudging such leaders can effect largescale behavioural change.

Of course, those in formal leadership roles toward the top of the organisational hierarchy are also in a good position to effect widespread behavioural change by altering organisational policies and procedures. Nudges that help high-level decision makers (leaders, boards, etc.) optimise organisational policy decisions in the face of their own biases and irrationalities can have an effect. Thus, helping decision makers see the connection between policies, procedures and behaviour on the ground is another way to nudge whole organisations.

Source: (OECD, 2020[23])

For example, an internal cultural change strategy within the CGR might include:

- The implementation of measures that aim at promoting day-to-day learning through superiors and peers, identifying and raising awareness among internal leaders who can become vectors of change.
- Internal communication and awareness raising about preventive control mechanisms.
- Establishing the internal performance objectives of preventive control. As mentioned above, these objectives ideally may not be associated with the number of "findings" or "alerts" issued, but rather with results in generating change in risk management within the public administration.
- Strengthening the preventive control groups within the Sectorial Delegate Comptrollers. In particular, establishing management of preventive control at the second level of the Delegate. This will mean that even when the auditor can act in both directions, the preventive function can be clearly differentiated both internally and externally.

The interviews conducted for this project also highlighted that preventive control does not only require a cultural change in the CGR. In addition, it will be very important to work, from the CGR and from the public administration, to achieve change among financial managers so that they understand and appropriate the support that the CGR can provide them without perceiving this to be co-administration. Continuing and nurturing the Bank of Good Fiscal Management Practices, not only to evaluate the management and results of the control subjects, but also to provide guidelines for proper fiscal management, will be essential for this purpose.

Preventive and concomitant control, through its potential to help identify risks in public entities, can also leverage cultural changes within public entities and help improve public governance. This is because preventive controls have the potential to promote transparency and strengthen accountability. Of course preventive controls can create tensions and critical reactions, especially when the consequences involve more work for the auditees. However, these progressive tensions may eventually be accepted if their recipients understand and see their work rewarded throughout the chain of public management, including the gradual improvement of public governance (Kimi Makwetu, 2020[24]).

To this end, it is recommended that the CGR and the Administrative Department of the Public Service (*Departamento Administrativo de la Función Pública*, DAFP) join forces to develop and implement measures that seek to explain and promote the acceptance of preventive control as an ally for the strengthening of public management. In addition, the CGR could analyse how, on its side, it can contribute to improving the relationship between auditors and auditees. For example, audit reports written in simpler and less technical-legal language could facilitate both ownership by the public administration and monitoring by citizens. Simpler language will make it easier to understand, increase motivation to act and eventually improve the impact of preventive control mechanisms.

References

Australian National Audit Office (2020), *Corporate Plan 2020-21*, https://www.anao.gov.au/work/corporate/anao-corporate-plan-2020-21. [10]

Bicchieri, C. (2017), *Norms in the wild: How to diagnose, measure, and change social norms*, http://dx.doi.org/10.1093/acprof:oso/9780190622046.001.0001. [19]

Bicchieri, C. (2005), *The grammar of society: The nature and dynamics of social norms*, http://dx.doi.org/10.1017/CBO9780511616037. [20]

CGR Perú (2015), *Estudio sobre las Causas y efectos de las renegociaciones contractuales de las Asociaciones Público - Privadas en el Perú*, Contraloría General de la República del Perú, Lima, https://library.pppknowledgelab.org/documents/2406/download (accessed on 24 September 2021). [14]

Contraloría General de la República de Colombia (2021), *Una Contraloría para Todos: informe de Gestión 2020-2021*. [2]

Court of Auditors (2019), *Public Audit in the European Union 2019 Edition*, https://op.europa.eu/webpub/eca/book-state-audit/en/ (accessed on 23 November 2021). [8]

DNP (2021), *CONPES 4045*, https://colaboracion.dnp.gov.co/CDT/Conpes/Econ%C3%B3micos/4045.pdf (accessed on 8 September 2021). [1]

EY (2015), *How big data and analytics are transforming the audit*, https://www.ey.com/en_lb/assurance/how-big-data-and-analytics-are-transforming-the-audit (accessed on 25 August 2021). [13]

Froy, F. and S. Giguère (2010), *Breaking Out of Policy Silos*, OECD, http://dx.doi.org/10.1787/9789264094987-en. [15]

Gepp, A. et al. (2018), "Big data techniques in auditing research and practice: Current trends and future opportunities", *Journal of Accounting Literature*, Vol. 40, pp. 102-115, http://dx.doi.org/10.1016/J.ACCLIT.2017.05.003. [12]

House of Commons, United Kingdom (2017), *Value for Money Study, Delivery of Benefits From the NAO's IT Enabled Change Program*, https://www.parliament.uk/globalassets/documents/public-accounts-commission/15-NAO-VFM-report-on-IT-enabled-change-programme.pdf. [7]

Inter-American Development Bank (2019), *Informe de Evaluación del Desempeño*, https://www.contraloria.gov.co/documents/20181/449782/Informe+Final+MMD+EFS+CGR+Colombia+2019_unlocked.pdf/611096c8-6eef-4de0-924e-2839eab84552 (accessed on 24 August 2021). [17]

INTOSAI (2019), "Data Analytics Guideline". [5]

INTOSAI (2019), *ISSAI 300*. [16]

Kimi Makwetu (2020), "Re-establishing accountability". [24]

Langhe, B. and S. Puntoni (2020), *Leading With Decision-Driven Data Analytics*, MIT Sloan Management Review, https://sloanreview.mit.edu/article/leading-with-decision-driven-data-analytics/ (accessed on 9 September 2021). [4]

OECD (2020), *Behavioural Insights and Organisations: Fostering Safety Culture*, OECD Publishing, Paris, https://dx.doi.org/10.1787/e6ef217d-en. [23]

OECD (2019), *Analytics for Integrity: Data-driven Approaches for Enhancing Corruption and Fraud Assessments*, OECD Publishing, Paris, http://www.oecd.org/gov/ethics/analytics-for-integrity.pdf. [3]

OECD (2019), *Tools and Ethics for Applied Behavioural Insights: The BASIC Toolkit*, OECD Publishing, Paris, https://dx.doi.org/10.1787/9ea76a8f-en. [22]

OECD (2018), *Behavioural Insights for Public Integrity: Harnessing the Human Factor to Counter Corruption*, OECD Public Governance Reviews, OECD Publishing, Paris, https://dx.doi.org/10.1787/9789264297067-en. [18]

OECD (forthcoming), *Analytics at Mexico's Supreme Audit Institution: Considerations and priorities for assessing integrity risks*, OECD Publishing, Paris. [11]

Revista do TCU (2016), "Evolution of Control in the", *Federal Court of Accounts Journal*, http://See PDF (accessed on 3 August 2021). [9]

U.K. National Audit Office (2019), *Transparency Report*, https://www.nao.org.uk/wp-content/uploads/2020/07/National-Audit-Office-Transparency-Report-2019-20.pdf. [6]

Yamin, P. et al. (2019), "sustainability Using Social Norms to Change Behavior and Increase Sustainability in the Real World: a Systematic Review of the Literature", *Sustainability*, Vol. 11/20, p. 5847, http://dx.doi.org/10.3390/su11205847. [21]

3 Strengthening co-ordination between the Office of the Comptroller General, the internal control system and citizens

This chapter identifies challenges and opportunities to ensure appropriate co-ordination between the external control and the internal and social control. In particular, it analyses how preventive and concomitant control can be better used as a tool to support the public administration, including through the relationship and feedback provided to fiscal managers and as an additional source of information for the public administration in the management of corruption risks.

The role of internal control in the preventive and concomitant control function: challenges and perspectives

The OECD Recommendation on Public Integrity emphasises the need to implement a framework for risk management and control that safeguards integrity in public sector entities (OECD, 2017[1]). The three lines of defence model helps distinguish the existence of three groups within a public organisation for effective risk management and control. By acting effectively, they can better ensure compliance with organisational objectives (OECD, 2019[2]). The Colombian model adopted a fourth line, which they called the "strategic line", taking into account the legal framework of internal control that expressly assigns responsibility for the system to the legal representative of the entity. Therefore, these representatives, as well as their management teams, constitute the fourth complementary line to the regular three-lines of defence scheme. The SAI, in turn, can be understood as a fifth line of defence, external to the public organisation, which complements the internal control systems and ensures their proper functioning and effective governance (Arndorfer and Minto, 2015[3]). For this, good co-ordination between the internal and external control systems is vital.

As regards internal control, the Internal Control Units (*Unidades de Control Interno, UCI*) play a fundamental role as advisor, evaluator, system integrator and energiser of the internal control system. These functions are aimed at improving the organisational culture and, therefore, contribute to the fulfilment of the purposes of the State. This is why the OECD Integrity Review of Colombia highlighted the challenges in strengthening co-ordination between the CGR, the DAFP and the Auditor General Office (*Auditoría General de la República*, AGR) and in particular the articulation, alignment and harmonisation of standards with respect to the internal control system (OECD, 2017[4]).

As such, Legislative Act 04 of 2019 and Decree 403 of 2020 (Art. 57 (c)) established a new role for the UCI for the preventive and concomitant control. In the CGR, the administration of the SACI was given to the Delegate for Citizen Participation to promote fluent communication between the UCI and the General and Sectorial Delegate Comptrollers' Offices to appropriately exchange information for the real time surveillance of public resources.

Moreover, the Internal Control System (Law 87 of 1993) is implemented for the public sector in Colombia under the Internal Control Standard Model (*Modelo Estandár de Control Interno, MECI*), which is composed of two elements: a control structure and a scheme for assigning responsibilities, called lines of defence (Decree 1083 of 2015 on the Institutional Internal Control Co-ordination System). Under the lines of defence scheme, the UCI are in charge of the third line of defence aimed at being the "control of controls". That is, the UCI verify and evaluate whether the controls implemented and monitored by the strategic line (senior management and the Institutional Internal Control Co-ordination Committee (*Comité Institucional de Coordinación de Control Interno, CICI*)), the first line of defence (leaders, process managers, collaborators) and the second line of defence (co-ordinators, planning offices and axis leaders) are implemented, applied and effective. Therefore, the UCI are only a part of the internal control system, not the system as a whole, among other reasons because based on the independence and objectivity to which they are bound, they are not permitted to be part of all of the processes of an institution.

The interviews conducted for this report revealed the need to improve co-ordination and the link between the UCI and the Office of the Comptroller General. The interaction between public entities and the CGR, for the purposes of preventive or concomitant control, is currently being defined and structured. For example, the interviews indicated that public administrations still follow a reactive logic to the observations of the CGR and that this also holds for the preventive and concomitant control, even when the law states explicitly that "warnings" are non-binding and entail no legal consequences. However, the UCI expressed doubts with respect to whether the warning system really does not have legal consequences. This may be a consequence of the fact that many associate the CGR to its traditional role related to sanctions. In addition, concerns about disparate criteria and the scope of the role of UCI in preventive control were confirmed, as well as opportunities for improvements in this new mechanism. The problems identified in the framework of this project are summarised below (Figure 3.1).

Figure 3.1. Perceptions of the UCI on preventive and concomitant control

CGR have a reactive vision and with difficult timescales to meet.	The internal areas of the CGR are independent and each one seeks different things.	The issue of real-time information is not fine-tuned. Criteria are unclear on what to report.	They do not submit a feedback report to the UCIs. There is a culture associated with UCIs only receiving the "flack".
Warnings are issued through the media.	New powers of the new control entity overwhelmed.	A procedure is urgently needed to make this preventive and concomitant control more organised.	Ignorance of the scope of the concomitant control by the UCIs, as well as by certain CGR officials
Lack of defined links.	Internal control is prioritised toward risks and sample works. There is no way to cover everything that the CGR requires.	CGR very focused on detecting cases of corruption, rather than prevention.	The territorial internal control offices are not empowered to respond effectively to the needs of the CGR.

Source: Focus group and interviews within the framework of the OECD-CGR project

Therefore, the concerns of the UCI about the application of preventive and concomitant control can be summarised into three areas for improvement.

- Improving CGR's co-ordination with internal control, including procedures and information requests.
- Strengthening the role of UCI in the identification and treatment of integrity risks, beyond the identification and notification of possible cases of corruption.
- Strengthening the UCI in its entirety, allocating the necessary resources and support for the fulfilment of their functions, including on the territorial level.

Improving CGR's co-ordination with internal control, including procedures and information requests

One of the main concerns identified by the UCI is undoubtedly related to their interaction with the CGR and the use and purpose of the information they produce. In particular, concerns were observed related to requests for information as well as the times and the applicable procedures for each process (alerts or warnings). A fundamental aspect unanimously highlighted was the idea of the CGR as a kind of "black box", to which they send information, but no feedback is received on its use or usefulness. Because of this, the interviewed actors considered it necessary to establish informal communication channels (such as feedback meetings) and to create clear links for the requests of information made to the UCI.

This interaction may enhance positive aspects discussed during the virtual fact-finding mission, which, among others, evidenced significant institutional changes. In particular, the UCI feel that even though there are aspects to be fine-tuned, overall there has been an important cultural change among CGR officials. Proof of this were the references to moving from a "scarier" to friendlier entity, which can use the UCI as a leverage to fulfil its role, with a strengthened legal framework and more modern work tools. In interviews conducted for this report, the UCI expressed the imperative need to potentiate this last point, since not only the technical and instrumental aspects are key to achieving the desired interaction, but also the attitudinal changes that have been perceived from the CGR auditors.

These efforts should be complemented with a better articulation with internal control. For example, articles 57 and 61 of Decree 403 of 2020 mention the need for co-ordination with internal control, but the CGR guidelines on how this co-ordination would occur are still pending, including at all levels of the control system, such as legal representatives, administrators and the *CICI*. As explained below, the modification of Resolution 49 of 2019 could be an opportunity to implement some of these recommendations and refine procedural aspects of this interaction, including identifying other co-ordination mechanisms and finding the limits and common points of each of the controls.

Strengthening the role of Internal Control Units in the management of integrity risks, beyond the identification and transfer of possible cases of corruption

Secondly, the UCI show concern in how the CGR understands their role in relation to the concomitant and preventive control. In particular, their role in the detection of corruption cases or their role in the internal control process, which, as already explained, is limited to the third line of defence and not to the whole system.

To this end, it is necessary to consider several points:

- The UCI exercise their roles and functions in accordance with their Annual Audit Plan and on prioritised topics based on risks.
- Internal audit is based on sampling and is aimed at evaluating processes, it is neither appropriate nor possible to evaluate the universe of contracts, projects or programmes, nor participate or intervene in institutional activity.
- The assessment that the UCI can provide, according to its competences, is carried out fundamentally in matters of risks, control and formulation of actions.
- The UCI evaluate the procurement process ensuring that it has controls throughout all its stages and that these controls are present in any selection process. For this, within the framework of an audit, "samples" are selected based on various modalities and in relation to different stages. This is given as input for the actions to be taken by the administration.

For this reason, the UCI cannot verify everything that happens in the contracts nor can they alert about all situations that arise. Furthermore, and as highlighted in the OECD Public Integrity Review of Colombia (OECD, 2017[4]), it is not their role to identify specific corruption cases (Box 3.1). In this sense, the Office of the Comptroller General could consider strengthening and giving a clearer perspective to the "alert" mechanism so it is not confused with the public "warnings" of the Comptroller General, making it clear that the "alerts" and what the SACI is intended for, is more aligned to the function of the UCI, which includes the identification of risks that jeopardises the achievement of the State's goals in the investment of public resources and that can generate loss or damage, rather than in the identification of specific corruption cases. As such, the UCI would have the potential to play a more proactive role by providing inputs or even supporting risk assessments with regards to the preventive control.

Box 3.1. Role of Internal Audit in Fraud and Corruption

It is not a primary role of internal audit to detect fraud and corruption. Internal audit's role is to provide an independent opinion based on an objective assessment of the framework of governance, risk management and control.

In doing so, internal auditors may:

- Review the organisation's risk assessment seeking evidence on which to base an opinion that fraud and corruption risks have been properly identified and responded to appropriately (i.e. within the risk appetite).

- Provide an independent opinion on the effectiveness of prevention and detection processes put in place to reduce the risk of fraud and/or corruption.

- Review new programmes and policies (and changes in existing policies and programmes) seeking evidence that the risk of fraud and corruption had been considered where appropriate and providing an opinion on the likely effectiveness of controls designed to reduce the risk.

- Consider the potential for fraud and corruption in every audit assignment and identify indicators that crime might have been committed or control weaknesses that might indicate a vulnerability to fraud or corruption.

- Review areas where major fraud or corruption has occurred to identify any system weaknesses that were exploited or controls that did not function properly and make recommendations about strengthening internal controls where appropriate.

- Assist with, or carry out investigations on management's behalf. Internal auditors should only investigate suspicious or actual cases of fraud or corruption if they have the appropriate expertise and understanding of relevant laws to allow them to undertake this work effectively. If investigation work is undertaken, management should be made aware that the internal auditor is acting outside of the core internal audit remit and of the likely impact on the audit plan.

- Provide an opinion on the likely effectiveness of the organisation's fraud and corruption risk strategy (e.g. policies, response plans, whistleblowing policy, codes of conduct) and if these have been communicated effectively across the organisation. Management has primary responsibility for ensuring that an appropriate strategy is in place and the role of internal audit is to review the effectiveness of the strategy.

Source: United Kingdom, HM Treasury (2012), Fraud and the Government Internal Auditor, January 2012.

Strengthening the UCI by assigning the necessary resources and providing support for the fulfilment of their functions, including on the territorial level

Strengthening the UCI, particularly in terms of resources and personnel, is not a new concept in Colombia. The OECD Public Integrity Review of Colombia has warned of the imperative need to allocate human, financial and technological resources needed for its proper functioning, as well as to promote the conditions for the independent development of its function (OECD, 2017[4]). This situation tends to worsen even more at the territorial level, where the UCI do not have the personnel or access to sufficient technology to carry out their tasks. In this sense, the situation seems not to have evolved much since the report produced by the OECD in 2017. This became even more evident during the interviews conducted for this report, where the UCI (on the national and territorial level) expressed that even though they are well aware of their obligation and commitment to contribute to the prevention of the loss of public resources, this task must be carried out in compliance with their functions and competences (which are not to identify specific cases of corruption) as well as considering their technical and human capacities.

To the limited allocation of budget and personal, there is an additional concern related to the lack of independence in the implementation of their functions, the high turnover of UCI heads and teams, as well as the excess of regulations and functions assigned to the unit. This situation does not allow consolidating an adequate management of controls or the possibility to permeate correctly through the different dependencies of an entity.

To overcome some of these challenges, the OECD Integrity review of Colombia had proposed, for example, that the DAFP explores the benefits of piloting a shared audit services model in a specific policy sector, for example, in the health sector or for local governments, as a strategy to strengthen internal control in local areas that have been affected by the armed conflict and as required by the Peace Agreement (OECD, 2017[4]). This recommendation could undoubtedly be taken up within the framework of the new preventive and concomitant control function, as well as in the process of unification and standardisation of the surveillance and control of fiscal management in Colombia, implementing, for example, initial pilots at the territorial level where UCI have limited resources to carry out their functions.

Role of the Citizen Participation Delegate to strengthen the relationship between the CGR and the Internal Control Units and to promote social control

As already mentioned, the Delegate for Citizen Participation (*Delegado de Participación Ciudadana, DPC*) plays a fundamental role in managing the SACI and works as a dependency that is constantly in communication with the DAFP. According to the DPC, the relationship with the UCI is determined in two spaces. On the one hand, the UCI play a role in accompanying the Participatory Fiscal Control (*Control Fiscal Participativo, CFP*), which is a service designed for citizens, so that they can exercise their right to monitor public management. In these institutional and social workshops, public entities, internal control units, contractors and citizens are invited to examine a problem related to the execution of national, regional or local projects. In these workshops, entities identify imminent or materialised risks in the development of a project and, with the aim to seek a solution and prompt completion, sign management agreements with the CGR. These agreement finalise once the good or service is delivered or when the execution of the process is restored.

On the other hand, since the issuance of Decree 403 of 2020 and Resolution 762 of 2020, the Delegate for Citizen Participation is also in charge of managing the SACI, understood as a communication mechanism with the UCI for monitoring the permanent implementation of preventive and concomitant control. Without a doubt, the creation of the SACI will contribute significantly to the exchange of information between the UCI and the CGR.

This constant interaction between the CGR and the UCI has been fundamental in the development of the preventive and concomitant control function, but some challenges remain. For instance, the UCI indicate inefficiencies between the reports to the multiple systems and platforms where records must be made, such as the system for reporting acts of corruption in charge of the Secretariat of Transparency of the Presidency of the Republic. This shows the importance and relevance of the SACI as an opportunity for the CGR to contribute to the co-ordination and unification of reporting systems.

The CGR also points out to challenges and opportunities. Among them stands out the difficulty encountered in the participation of the UCI when invited by the CGR for the purposes of Participatory Fiscal Control, since, according to the CGR, its vision is centred on the fact that interaction with citizens must always be mediated by the Citizen Service System (*Sistema de Servicio al Ciudadano*) that the entity in question has implemented. In addition, there is no feedback by the UCI on the comments made by citizens or whether the UCI follow up on actions implemented by the entities following their accountability processes.

As such, the interviews conducted for this report revealed a need to leverage the role of the Delegate for Citizen Participation and provide it with a more leading role in relation to the empowerment of citizens, which would facilitate to incorporate a citizen-based approach into the work of the CGR and the UCI. For the purposes of consolidating these actions, the CGR is developing the modification of Resolution 49 of 2019 to adapt and strengthen the Participatory Fiscal Control System.

Notwithstanding said reform, the CGR could also consider taking the following actions, in the way it deems best, to clarify and provide the scope for preventive and concomitant control and particularly its relationship with the UCI and with the general public:

- Strengthen and give a clearer perspective to early alerts so that they are not confused with the public warnings of the Comptroller General.

- Clarify the role of the UCI in relation to identifying early alerts in the context of the preventive and concomitant control, taking into consideration the limits of their role and functions, in particular with respect to their contributions to the identification of specific acts of corruption.

- Incorporate the information produced via "alerts" or "warnings" as an additional element for planning internal audits, in particular through giving feedback to the UCI. This will allow better decision making in the identification of processes and auditable units within the entities, as well as improving interaction between the parties. Therefore, even when is clear that the CGR should not give feedback to the UCI on internal work documents (since these are confidential), it can give feedback to the UCI related to the information provided by them and the risk analysis conducted based on the information provided by them.

- Create adequate communication channels with the UCI in order to fine-tune the co-operation mechanisms, so that requests for information from the UCI are streamlined and requests for the same documents by multiple units of the CGR are avoided. This could be achieved, for example through a strengthening of the Integrated Planning and Management Model (*Modelo Integrado de Planeación y Gestión*, MIPG) and the MECI regarding the identification of fiscal risks, as well as through clear guidelines on risk management with a focus on fraud and corruption.

- Generate citizen empowerment processes and more clearly establish their role in the context of the preventive and concomitant control. The CGR must consider citizens not only as a source of information on specific cases, but to whom accountability is given on the use and results of preventive and concomitant control. This would imply a cultural change in which the CGR is not seen as a "black box", where information from the citizen only enters, but a "glass box", where all the processes and procedures associated with preventive and concomitant control can be followed up on, respecting the due limitations of some of the processes or information. To this end, the CGR could make more visible certain actions taken to generate alerts, the processes and organisation charts associated with preventive control, as well as the indicators mentioned in Chapter 1 related to the improvement of processes of public entities.

- The Delegate for Citizen Participation could promote collaboration agreements between social organisations, including universities and the CGR to collaborate in citizen technology initiatives and empower citizens as partners in the promotion of open data.

- The Delegate for Citizen Participation could, based on alerts issued, prepare risk maps made available to citizens and allow their feedback, including on how to make use of these tools and information.

- Co-ordinate the CGR's existing information systems to be able to identify risks that have materialised and which should be known by all public institutions with the aim of using them as example in the review and update of risk maps and to strengthen controls. Said information could have a filter, so that the integrity of the investigation in progress is not affected, but ensuring that the information serves as a preventive alert to avoid damage and impact to public resources in other entities.

- Conduct feedback processes with UCI on the quality of the information they collect and produce.
- The Office of the Auditor General may be invited to take part in the actions to strengthen the two controls and, in particular, make use of the information it produces through its "red flag" system.

Finally, the implementation of the SACI is urgent, as it will contribute significantly to the exchange of information between the UCI and the CGR. To this end, the CGR and the DAFP have been working on a joint circular addressed to the heads of internal control, or those who act as such, of any level and that execute national public resources, establishing guidelines for the implementation of mechanisms for the articulation of external fiscal control with the entities' internal fiscal control through the SACI. The CGR has made progress in this task, since for the issuance of the aforementioned circular, multiple working groups have been held between teams from the CGR and the DAFP, seeking to clarify and define the scope that the SACI should have with regard to the public entities that, as a general rule, are not subject to control by the CGR, discussing as well whether the SACI should become fully operational at once or whether it is necessary to first implement pilots to be able to identify points for improvement and adjustment..

References

Arndorfer, I. and A. Minto (2015), "The "four lines of defence model" for financial institutions: Taking the three-lines-of-defence model further to reflect specific governance features of regulated financial institutions Isabella Arndorfer Bank for International Settlements", http://www.bis.org (accessed on 27 September 2021). [3]

OECD (2019), *La Integridad Pública en América Latina y el Caribe 2018-2019: De Gobiernos reactivos a Estados proactivos*, OECD, Paris, https://www.oecd.org/gov/integridad/integridad-publica-en-america-latina-caribe-2018-2019.htm. [2]

OECD (2017), *OECD Integrity Review of Colombia: Investing in Integrity for Peace and Prosperity*, OECD Public Governance Reviews, OECD Publishing, Paris, https://dx.doi.org/10.1787/9789264278325-en. [4]

OECD (2017), *OECD Recommendation on Public Integrity*, OECD, Paris, https://www.oecd.org/gov/ethics/OECD-Recommendation-Public-Integrity.pdf. [1]

4 Towards a fiscal management public policy in Colombia

This chapter offers a long-term vision for fiscal control in Colombia. It focuses on how such a vision could help ensuring the co-ordination and continuity of preventive and concomitant control in Colombia. In particular, co-ordination mechanisms as well as planning and policy tools such as the National Development Plan (NDP), the National Moralisation Commission (CNM), the Regional Moralisation Commissions (CRM) and others can contribute to the strengthening and continuity of preventive and concomitant control.

Ensure the co-ordination and continuity of preventive control in Colombia through a fiscal management public policy

Ensuring the co-ordination and continuity of preventive control in Colombia through a public fiscal management policy is essential. In particular, it is necessary to ensure that any public policy reform is influenced by technical aspects and the needs of modern and efficient fiscal management and control. A fiscal management public policy must be aligned with current international practices, including by migrating to a fiscal management capable of giving constructive recommendations to the public administration or making effective and efficient use of data analytics.

A reform could be sought to allow progress towards a fiscal management aligned with international practices, which contributes to the development of improvement processes in Colombia's public management. This reform could include aspects related to the continuity of internal processes, for example by including a policy vision that exceeds the 4-year period currently assigned to an administration. In essence, the preventive and concomitant control of the CGR should be part of a State policy that allows a long-term vision of its aims and objectives.

As such, the CGR can benefit from existing co-ordination spaces, which may help to leverage trust within public administration entities. Among them, Law of 2020 of 2016 created the Colombian "National Integrity System" to promote the concurrence of all State entities, the private sector and citizens around the promotion of integrity in the Colombian public service. This system includes a co-ordinating committee which includes the National Moralisation Commission (*Comisión Nacional de Moralización*, CNM) and the Regional Moralisation Commissions (*Comisiones Regionales de Moralización*, CRM) and entrusts the Administrative Department of the Public Service (DAFP) with its operation. Taking into account the need to use existing co-ordination spaces that strengthen the management of fiscal control, as well as the importance of promoting cultural change around preventive and concomitant control, the CGR may consider using its interaction with these bodies to promote its tools for corruption risk management.

Promote the inclusion of a long-term vision of fiscal control in Colombia in the next National Development Plan, including issues related to preventive and concomitant control as well as tools to strengthen the institutional image of the CGR among citizens

According to the CGR, the instruments currently used by the CGR aimed at the long-term vision of fiscal control are those of institutional planning, such as the entity's action plan and the applicable legal framework. However, several previous studies recommended to have a unification and standardisation of surveillance and control in Colombia through a public policy that guides long-term objectives (Inter-American Development Bank, 2019[1]).

The previous purposes were specified in the National Development Plan (PND) 2018-2022, which establishes the need for hierarchical and functional restructuring of some dependencies of the CGR. Thus, the PND 2018-2022 establishes that for the purposes of the surveillance of national and territorial fiscal management:

> "The Presidency of the Republic will lead the process of restructuring the model of national and territorial fiscal control, in co-ordination with all the competent entities, to guarantee professionalisation in the preventive and warning functions that allow the co-ordination and timely restitution of damages to public assets. This model must take into account the financial and managerial/administrative autonomy of territorial fiscal control, the selection by merit of the territorial comptrollers, the change of periods that foresee the interference of local actors, the adoption of anti-clientelistic measures and the possibility of investing in technology and institutional modernisation." (Departamento Nacional de Planeacion, 2018[2])

To this end, the purpose of the government's policy for the period 2018-2022 corresponds, on the one hand, to restructuring the surveillance model developed by both the CGR and the Territorial Comptrollers'

Offices, so that it is carried out from the perspective of the prevention of fiscal damage, with the professionalisation and specialisation of these entities. On the other hand, the purposes of the policy requires providing financial and administrative autonomy to fiscal control agencies, modifying the election periods of territorial comptrollers and the possibility for these bodies to strengthen investments in technological improvement. The PND 2018-2022 allowed the President of the Republic to hierarchically and functionally restructure the CGR, including the creation of several new Delegates and the creation of the DIARI.

As such, several legal and institutional changes have led to the need for a public policy related to fiscal management. The reform established 3 966 new control subjects of the territorial order, upon which the CGR will have the power to carry out a preventive or concomitant control at its discretion. In practice, this reform entails moving from a universe of 1 711 control subjects to a new potential scenario of 5 677 subjects and represents a drastic change in the CGR's scope of action. Although the institution has wide territorial deployment, since in addition of 31 Departmental Management Offices, it had never exercised control over territorial entities (DNP, 2021[3]).

These conditions generate the need to establish a public policy that allows the development of the full potential of the CGR, including by providing feedback to the public administration and that answers to the challenges established by this novel reform. In addition to this challenge, the 2019 reform established that the CGR must direct and implement the National System of Fiscal Control, with the support of the General Auditor of the Republic and that this must achieve the unification and standardisation of the surveillance and control of fiscal management in the country.

This policy could contain the unified vision of preventive and concomitant control, as well as tools for the strengthening and institutionalisation of other functions of the CGR. International examples, such as Mexico, show the advantages of having a national control system as a complement to the national anti-corruption public policy (Box 4.1).

Box 4.1. National Fiscal System (SNF) in Mexico

In May 2015, the Mexican Congress approved a set of governance reforms to improve the accountability, integrity and transparency of the public sector. These measures, which in some cases implied reforms to the country's Constitution, drew a new map of national institutions to promote the creation of the National Anti-Corruption System and the National Transparency System.

Part of the reforms focused on expanding the mandate of the Audit Office of the Federation (*Auditoría Superior de la Federación*, ASF) and providing it with additional tools to carry out its work, for example, the ability to carry out real-time audits, conduct investigations and report more frequently to Congress. The effectiveness of the National Audit System and the recent reforms also depend on other participants, such as the Ministry of the Public Function (*Secretaria de Función Pública*, SFP) - the federal entity responsible for internal control - as well as sub-national government audit bodies, where legal frameworks, capacities, resources and needs are different.

The operational bases for the operation of the National Audit System also establish a set of inter-institutional co-ordination mechanisms between the bodies responsible for audits in the different levels of government. The aim is to maximise the coverage and impact of the audit throughout the country, based on a strategic vision, the application of similar professional standards, the creation of capacities and the effective exchange of information, without duplications or omissions.

Source: (OECD, 2017[4])

Issues such as institutional continuity may require a reduction of auditor turnover and promulgating specialisation among auditors, including General, Sectorial and Territorial Delegate Comptrollers and senior managers. To this end, the possibility of extending the management period of the Comptroller General of the Republic may even be considered, to avoid administrative and personnel changes every 4 years. In matters of legislative reform, a legislative proposal that aims to allow the CGR to issue recommendations to public entities could be considered, clarifying the difference between constructive recommendations and co-administration and alongside this, empowering Departmental managers in all fiscal control cycles, with special emphasis on the role they play in preventive and concomitant control.

Furthermore, a long-term vision should include an analysis of the opportunities and challenges related to the role of the Comptroller towards external actors. To this end, the CGR could think of designing a public policy that goes beyond the 4 years of the PND and that guides the actions of the entire sector. In particular, this policy, which could be designed as a 10-year Plan for Fiscal Management, would have the potential to promote trust, accountability and improved information to citizens regarding the role of the CGR as guarantor of public finances.

With regard to preventive and concomitant control, several academics and members of civil society expressed the need to know more in detail about this long-term vision of the CGR, as well as procedural aspects of the mechanism, including its functioning, advantages and disadvantages, as well as the need to generate technical criteria that allow social control over it. The CGR could then make methodological aspects and the results of this very new control, much more visible.

To this end, the CGR could consider implementing actions within this policy aimed at making the internal structure associated with preventive and concomitant control more visible, as well as displaying its more technical aspects, such as, for example, its contributions to risk management within public entities or its role in data governance in Colombia. For this purpose, it is also essential to launch the General Public Warning System (SIGAP), administered by the Planning Office of the CGR that has not yet been completed; and seek progress in the bank of positive results tied to this system, as well as the bank of good fiscal management practices.

Make use of the National Moralisation Commission and the Regional Moralisation Commissions as spaces for co-ordination with the public administration and in relation to fiscal management in Colombia

In Colombia, the National Moralisation Commission (CNM) is a high-level mechanism that works for co-ordination between relevant actors to prevent and combat corruption. The CNM currently has 13 members; among them the President of the Republic; the Prosecutor General; the Attorney General and the Comptroller General. The Transparency Secretariat of the Vice Presidency of the Republic is the technical secretary of the CNM. The CNM must ensure the exchange of information and data between the aforementioned organisations, establish indicators to evaluate transparency in public administration and adopt an annual strategy to promote ethical conduct in the public administration. The CNM issues reports and publishes the minutes of the meetings (OECD, 2017[5]).

The OECD Public Integrity Review of Colombia had already emphasised the advantages of aligning and strengthening regulatory and integrity policies in Colombia through the National Moralisation Commission. The report pointed out that ensuring close co-ordination between the application of the law and integrity breaches prevention is key (OECD, 2017[5]).

As highlighted in this report, the need to demystify the work of the CGR and in particular its relationship with the public administration is imperative. To this end, the CNM has served as a communication channel on positive aspects and advantages of preventive and concomitant control, as well as a space for discussion on the doubts and objections of the executive branch. Indeed, the CNM has been a propitious setting to show the results of preventive and concomitant fiscal control, giving tools and information to the other members. An example of this have been the sessions held in 2021, where the CGR participated in the CNM, proposing the use of preventive and concomitant control to follow-up on resources used within the COVID-19 pandemic, in particular the purchase of vaccines and resources of the FOME (Emergency Mitigation Fund). At this meeting, the joint strategy with the Inspector General's Office (*Procuraduría General de la Nacion, PGN*) was presented. Moreover, issues related to concomitant and preventive control were discussed, such as the identification of critical projects or unfinished works and "white elephants". As such, "*Controlapp*" was presented as a tool for citizen control and reporting. This app allows to follow-up on projects intervened by preventive and concomitant control, such as the Túnel de la Línea, the Ruta del Soland the Orito-Putumayo Sewerage System, among others. This practice is a good example for the constructive use of the CNM as a platform for dialogue and the CGR should aim to continue in this direction.

On the territorial level, the CNM provides guidelines to be implemented by the Regional Moralisation Commissions (CRM) across the regions. In fact, the risks of corruption on the territorial level, compared to the national level, are often different and could be higher for various reasons (OECD, 2021[6]):

- First, a significant proportion of public resources are executed at territorial levels and sub-national governments have the responsibility for the provision of a large part of public services (such as water and sanitation, waste management, licenses and permits, education, health care etc.), which come along with risks to integrity (OECD, 2018[7]).

- Second, the territory of Colombia is often characterised by a greater weakness of external control. Territorial comptrollers' offices sometimes fail to escape the political logic of the regions and run a risk of being captured (OECD, 2021[6]). Regional political dynamics are evident in the elections of the territorial comptrollers, undermining the independence of these control bodies (Corredor and Cortés, 2018[8]). Several discussions have proposed to implement another election model that allows to uncouple these positions from political influences and to promote their professionalisation.

- Third, it was observed that at the sub-national level there are still gaps related to the qualification and capacity of the technical personnel of the territorial control bodies. Taking into consideration that this new preventive and concomitant control is based on the technical capacity of the teams, these deficiencies imply a risk for its success.

In the territory, the CRM are co-ordinating bodies for the fight against corruption and include regional representatives of the Inspector General (*Procuraduria General de la Nación*), the Prosecutor General (*Fiscalia General de la Nación*), the Comptroller General (*CGR*) and the Council of the Judiciary (*Consejo Seccional de la Judicatura*) as well as the Departmental, Municipal and District Comptrollers (*Contraloría Departamental, Municipal y Distrital*). The CRM are in charge of investigating, preventing and sanctioning corruption in the regions. In addition, other entities can be invited to the CRM when deemed necessary. Together with the CNM, they are part of the Co-ordination Committee of the National Integrity System created by Law 2016 of 2020.

The OECD report on CRM highlighted that, currently, the role of CRM in preventing corruption and fraud at the regional level is limited because they are not well co-ordinated with governments and municipalities (OECD, 2021[6]). Thus, the report recommends considering the expansion of the CRM to include the public administration as members and thus facilitate better co-ordination and dialogue. In the short term, periodic meetings between the CRMs and the regional governments could be promoted. Legislation already contemplates the possibility of inviting Governors and these meetings could be promoted with the support of the Transparency Secretariat and the DAFP on a semi-annual basis. The purpose of these regular interactions is, for example, to share ideas about corruption risks, establish priorities for the department, present progress made in the area of integrity and the fight against corruption and analyse opportunities for action as well as encountered challenges (OECD, 2021[6]).

It is in this framework that the perspective of the new preventive and concomitant control could be particularly conducive to improving the constructive dialogue between the CGR and local administrations. The CGR could make use of the spaces provided by the CRM to make visible the advantages of preventive and concomitant control but also use them as a source of feedback on patterns detected or alerts identified at the territorial level and could even consider passing this information to local administrations to act on it. An example for such a co-ordination, reported during the virtual fact finding mission, is in La Guajira, where an alert was shared by the CRM with the public administration, allowing a follow-up by the latter. This shows the potential for the CRMs to co-ordinate with governors and mayors.

References

Corredor, F. and V. Cortés (2018), "¿Por qué la presencia de las contralorías no disminuye la corrupción en Colombia?", in Henao Pérez, J. and C. Isaza Espinosa (eds.), *Corrupción, política y sociedad*, Universidad Externado de Colombia, Bogotá. [8]

Departamento Nacional de Planeacion (2018), *Plan Nacional de Desarrollo 2018-2022*, https://colaboracion.dnp.gov.co/CDT/Prensa/Resumen-PND2018-2022-final.pdf (accessed on 24 August 2021). [2]

DNP (2021), *CONPES 4045*, https://colaboracion.dnp.gov.co/CDT/Conpes/Econ%C3%B3micos/4045.pdf (accessed on 8 September 2021). [3]

Inter-American Development Bank (2019), *Informe de Evaluación del Desempeño*, https://www.contraloria.gov.co/documents/20181/449782/Informe+Final+MMD+EFS+CGR+Colombia+2019_unlocked.pdf/611096c8-6eef-4de0-924e-2839eab84552 (accessed on 24 August 2021). [1]

OECD (2021), *La Integridad Pública a Nivel Regional en Colombia: Empoderando a las Comisiones Regionales de Moralización*, OECD, Paris, http://www.oecd.org/corruption/ethics/integridad-publica-nivel-regional-colombia.pdf (accessed on 25 July 2021). [6]

OECD (2018), *Integrity for Good Governance in Latin America and the Caribbean: From Commitments to Action*, OECD Publishing, Paris, https://dx.doi.org/10.1787/9789264201866-en. [7]

OECD (2017), *Mexico's National Auditing System: Strengthening Accountable Governance*, OECD Public Governance Reviews, OECD Publishing, Paris, https://dx.doi.org/10.1787/9789264264748-en. [4]

OECD (2017), *OECD Integrity Review of Colombia: Investing in Integrity for Peace and Prosperity*, OECD Public Governance Reviews, OECD Publishing, Paris, https://dx.doi.org/10.1787/9789264278325-en. [5]

5 Recommendations to strengthen the implementation of preventive and concomitant control in Colombia

To facilitate discussions in the Office of the Comptroller General based on this report and its recommendations, the following table provides an overview of the actions proposed in the different chapters. Some recommended actions could be implemented in the short term and under the direct control of the Office of the Comptroller General, others may require a dialogue at the State level as well as legislative changes and could be considered as objectives in the medium or long term.

Chapter 1	Expand and train the existing normative body, including the internal regulations of the CGR related to the processes and procedures associated with alerts and warnings, emphasising the differences and functionalities of each one.
	Consider the unification of normative instruments (Decrees, Resolutions and Executive Regulatory Resolutions) into a single normative body and the unification of terms and concepts (e.g. the difference between early warnings issued by the CGR and early warnings issued by internal control) that help to clarify the role and functionalities of the different stages of the process.
	Generate an audit guide or an illustrative booklet aimed at entities, Departmental management and dependencies of the CGR where the operation of the two mechanisms and the actors that intervene in each one is explained, through examples and case studies, including examples of which actions may constitute co-administration and which are specific to preventive and concomitant control.
	Consider opening a dialogue at the State level in view of incorporating the possibility for the CGR to generate constructive recommendations to public administrations on how to address and mitigate the risks or problems identified in audits or during preventive control.
	Assertively measure the achievements and results of the preventive and concomitant control of the Comptroller's Office, incorporating the use of indicators that measure impacts with respect to structural changes in public administration.
	Consider establishing checks and balances in decision making regarding the warning mechanism. In particular, analyse the possibility of including with the publication of the warning supporting documents or a synthesis of the decision-making process, as well as a space for internal deliberation within the CGR that supports the final decision issued by the Comptroller General.
Chapter 2	Consider measuring the progress of the quality of data received and incorporating said component into the methodology of the Data Governance Model currently being designed.
	Promote, via the technical talks with the public administration and based on the technologies used by DIARI, the standardisation of a database model that allows the interoperability of high volumes of information, in such a way as to facilitate its automation.
	Continue joint work with the Office of the Attorney General of the Nation to achieve greater diligence on the part of the agencies that regulate public spending in the management and loading of fiscal management information.
	Promote, through the current interaction spaces (work tables and feedback reports), the automation by the entities of all their processes, in order to be able to have structured and better quality information.
	Work on the cleaning of data and feedback with other actors, including at the territorial level, private administrators and parafiscal funds.
	Communicate not only internally, but externally, the role of the "Data and Information Governance Committee" in such a way that it helps in the unification of the same technological standard in all Comptrollers, to facilitate the interaction of internal data.
	Based on the model of the CGR's Data Governance Committee, ensure that the public administration determines the design and implementation of an intersectorial committee (governing body) for the management and quality of data for all entities.
	Develop a unified view for data and analytics, including one that reflects audit and governance trends related to big data. This policy vision can be included and aligned with the next National Development Plan, providing broader goals for digital transformation.
	Establish indicators and a theory of change regarding data and analysis, focusing on results and not simply output (for example, indicators that reflect prevention, mitigation or recovery of loss).
	Develop an action plan to ensure the relevance of analytical initiatives and the reliability of results, particularly for new methodologies and systems under development.
	Use the data governance framework to help establish key areas to focus on and identify priorities.
	Incorporate tools aimed at preventive work, including the identification of risks in public administration, as well as the adequate communication thereof to financial managers. This work can in turn leverage the use of prospective models and incorporate information available within the different areas of the CGR (such as that produced, for example, by performance audits and sectorial studies).
	Promote learning, inclusion and experimentation by using data and new techniques, including developing a baseline to measure the impact of the CGR in relation to the new data analytics strategies and with regard to the results and advantages thereof.
	Raise awareness among CGR officials about data analytics and how it contributes to risk analysis in order to develop technical capacities and promote staff specialisation.
	Generate internal co-ordination through meetings between the DIARI and the General, Sectorial and Territorial Delegate Comptrollers' Offices in order to identify and make use of the internal information from the Comptroller's Office, including audit reports from previous years.
	Co-ordinate with the territorial level in such a way that they receive the same information shared with other dependencies of the CGR, in particular through the generation of links and the strengthening of capacities in the Departmental Management Offices.
	Take advantage of the new preventive and concomitant control to strengthen sectorial studies and performance audits.
	Encourage a behavioural and cultural change, leveraged on the current institutional framework of the CGR, which helps to understand and internalise the preventive function in the CGR in public administration and citizenship.

Include case study guides from previous exercises, as well as some international practices in the matter, in the permanent monitoring procedure public resources for the exercise of concomitant and preventive fiscal control (Process VIG 01 PR 001).

Analyse the possibility of having an internal, non-binding committee where some of the most relevant cases, risks identified and best ways to approximate the different situations would be discussed. In particular, this committee could count on input not only from the areas directly involved, but also from other relevant actors where applicable.

Continue with the feedback exercises of the DIARI to General, Sectorial and Territorial Delegate Comptrollers related to the usefulness, relevance and usage of the information they produce.

The DIARI could have closer communication with different areas of the CGR, including the Departmental Management Offices, via the sending of analysis reports they produce, as well as by providing training to them on the use and interpretation of the information produced.

Analyse the possibility of creating a specialised unit to allow the intersectoral analysis of the information collected by the Sectorial Delegate Comptrollers for the purposes of preventive and concomitant control.

Consider establishing concomitant and preventive control working groups as provided in Art. 38 of Resolution 762 of 2020 and in accordance with the needs of the CGR and the Sectorial Comptrollers' Offices.

Give the role of performing audits to the DES, as part of the process of evaluating public policies, which today is conducted by the DES themselves, ensuring co-ordination with the fiscal surveillance areas as appropriate..

Advance in updating the new Performance Audit Guide which incorporates the criteria and standards of ISSAIS 300 (3000, 3910, 3920) and Law Decree 403 of 2020.

Re-establish and restore the profiles required in the DES, in particular to provide the missing information related to performance audits.

Consolidate a team of mentors to carry out training programmes in performance audits, ensuring that those who receive the training have the appropriate profile for said functions.

Develop a strategy for citizen participation and that in turn contributes to the ODSs through mechanisms of dialogue, participation and accountability with citizens, which reflect a citizen vision for control and provide sustainability to audited public policies.

Continue training the General, Sectorial and Territorial Delegate Comptrollers Offices on the scope of preventive and concomitant control, as well as the use of the information produced by the DIARI. This could even be extended to risk analysis and public administration management, examining the capacity of the public administration to achieve the expected results.

Make use of the Centre for Fiscal Studies (CEF), which is in charge of high-quality training in matters of surveillance and control for the management of public resources, in to carry out internal training processes conducive to generating periodic programmes of the tasks of preventive control, including in the identification and management of corruption risks.

Consider implementing measures aimed at day-to-day learning via superiors and peers, identifying and raising awareness among internal leaders who can become vectors of change.

Establish the internal performance objectives of preventive control, which at the moment do not have a methodology to be measured.

Strengthen the preventive control groups within the Sectorial Delegate Comptrollers Offices. In particular, establish management of preventive control at the second level of the Delegate. This will mean that even when the auditor may act in both directions, the preventive function is clearly differentiated both internally and externally.

| Chapter 3 | Clarify the role of the UCIs in relation to identifying early warnings for preventive and concomitant control, taking into consideration the limits of their role and functions, in particular, the contributions in the identification of specific acts of corruption. |

Incorporate the information produced by "alerts" or "warnings" as additional elements for planning internal audits, in particular through feedback to the UCI.

Create adequate communication channels with the UCI in order to fine-tune co-operation mechanisms, so that requests for information from the UCIs are streamlined and requests for the same documents by multiple units of the CGR are avoided

Generate citizen empowerment processes and establish their role in preventive and concomitant control more clearly.

Make certain actions taken to generate alerts, processes and organisation charts associated with preventive control more visible.

Promote collaboration agreements between social organisations, including universities and the CGR to collaborate in citizen technology initiatives or rely on external control activities and empower citizens as partners in the promotion of open data.

Share the risks identified with public entities and agencies to serve as examples for reviewing risk maps, updating them and strengthening controls; as a source of knowledge and preventive mechanism for entities

Conduct feedback processes to UCIs on the quality of the information collected and produced by them.

The Office of the Auditor General of the Republic may be invited to take part in the actions to strengthen the two controls and, in particular, make use of the information it produces through the "red flag" system.

Continue with the creation of the SACI, as a source of support for the exchange of information between the UCIs and the CGR.

	Strengthen the Internal Control Units in their entirety, assigning the necessary resources and support for the fulfilment of their functions, including on the territorial level
Chapter 4	Ensure the co-ordination and continuity of preventive control in Colombia through a public policy of fiscal management.
	Include a long-term vision on fiscal control in Colombia in the next National Development Plan, including aspects related to preventive and concomitant control, as well as tools to strengthen the institutional image of the CGR among citizens.
	Promote exercises of institutional continuity that promote the reduction of auditor rotation and promote specialisation among them, including in General, Sectorial and Territorial Delegate Comptrollers and senior managers.
	Consider the possibility of extending the management period of the Comptroller General of the Republic to avoid administrative and personnel changes every 4 years.
	Empower the Departmental Management Offices in all fiscal control cycles, with special emphasis on the role they play in preventive and concomitant control
	Consider a public policy that even goes beyond the 4 years of the PND and guides the actions of the entire sector. In particular, this policy could be designed as a Ten-Year Plan for Fiscal Management,
	Consider making the internal structure associated with preventive and concomitant control more visible, as well as visualising its more technical aspects.
	Put the General Public Warning System (SIGAP) into operation.
	Make use of the National and Regional Moralisation Commissions as spaces for co-ordination with the public administration with regard to fiscal management in Colombia.
	Make use of the spaces provided by the CRM not only to make the advantages of preventive and concomitant control visible but also to use them as a source of feedback to the executive branch on patterns detected or alerts identified on the territorial level.

www.ingramcontent.com/pod-product-compliance
Lightning Source LLC
Chambersburg PA
CBHW080003280326
41935CB00013B/1737